MY GREEK KITCHEN

MY GREEK KITCHEN

MARY VALLE

Steven, Catherine, Rebecca and Sarah.
This is for you.

My fondest memories of growing up in a Greek family are of the laughter we shared, the conversations with loved ones, and enjoying good food in a warm-hearted home. The kitchen was the place where family stories were shared and many memories were made; a place to give advice, to reminisce, to discuss the future and a place where meals were created.

I remember our tiny kitchen, decorated with lace tablecloths and vases filled with flowers from our garden. It was splashed with colour, with pots and baking trays cluttering the stove. A corner of the kitchen was set aside for my mother's Greek Orthodox icons, where she would light a tiny candle on Sundays and festive days. The distinctive waxy smell would linger in the house long after the candle was blown out.

I clearly remember the fragrance of the oregano that my mother grew in the garden and then air-dried in bunches, later filling small jars with it. And, of course, there was the almost constant aroma of Greek coffee brewing on the stove; it seemed that my mother was always making coffee, and my father always drinking it.

Greek food plays a big role in my kitchen too. I have collected many recipes over the years. Some, I remember from my childhood and have adapted to modern times, many are from my travels to Greece where I have spent time over the last few years, and others are ones I simply love to cook for my family. I have been inspired by my travels and by watching people cook. Travel has enabled me to bring layers of Mediterranean/Aegean cooking from my experiences back into my own kitchen.

This collage of Greek food consists of the best vegetables grilled simply with a drizzle of olive oil, a squeeze of lemon and a sprinkling of oregano; creamy yogurt with the irresistible sweetness of honey; lamb roasts in spring and pork casseroles in winter. Fresh fruit and vegetables ripened under the sun, the emphasis being on seasonal foods ... and cooking in harmony with nature.

Like my mother, I taste as I cook and adapt recipes to suit my palate. Don't be afraid to develop your own versions of the dishes in this book, throw in your favourite ingredients and taste as you go. A pinch of this and a touch of that. There is nothing like losing yourself in the joys of making food.

Family, friends, laughter and the pleasure of simple, fresh meals can be so easily forgotten in our busy lives. Time passes so quickly, but these are the things that make memories: memories that I want my children to reminisce over.

I hope these recipes find a place in your home and your heart too.

Contents

Scrambled eggs with
  roasted red capsicum 60

Patatokeftethes
  (potato croquettes) 63

Soups 67

Yiouverlakia soup (meatball soup
  with egg and lemon sauce) 70

Fasolada (Greek bean soup) 72

Chicken soup avgolemeno 73

Lentil soup 75

Fish soup avgolemono 76

Revithada (chickpea soup) 80

Main Meals 85

Yemista (stuffed red capsicums)
  88

Pastitso 91

Moussaka 94

Dolmades (stuffed cabbage
  leaves) 98

Lamb and lettuce fricassée 100

Classic Greek lamb 103

Lemon and oregano potatoes 104

Lamb and okra casserole 105

Pork and celery avgolemono 108

Pork with leeks 109

Baked fish 110

Grilled lamb cutlets 115

Braised cauliflower with
  tomato and smoked
  sweet paprika 116

Greek roast pork 118

Roast potatoes with tomato 119

Lamb and macaroni
  casserole 121

Oven-baked chicken and
  rice 122

Baccala with skordalia 125

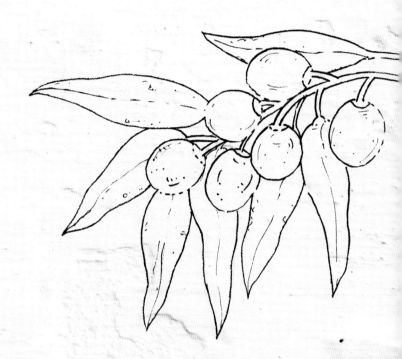

Desserts 211

My kitchen store cupboard is tall with double doors – not too big, though I would love an entire room that I could fill with the ingredients I adore. Below is a list of the typical ingredients that every Greek kitchen has, many are easily found and probably already in your pantry. Add seasonal fruit and vegetables, bought fresh, and any specialty ingredients as required.

The Greek Pantry

Feta cheese

Olive oil – extra virgin olive oil for salads and dressing and an everyday olive oil for cooking

Vinegar

Olives

Lemons

Herbs, spices and flavourings – dried oregano, bay leaves, sweet paprika, cinnamon, sea salt, black peppercorns, dill and parsley

Honey

Filo pastry

Flour – self-raising (self-rising) and plain (all-purpose)

Legumes – cannellini (white) beans, lentils, chickpeas (dried and canned)

Greek coffee

Ouzo

Dried pasta, rice, risoni

Sugar – caster (superfine) sugar and icing (confectioners') sugar

Bottles of tomato passata

Eggs

Greek (strained plain) yogurt

Jars of sweet preserves

Seasonal fruit and vegetables

Onions, garlic, carrots and celery

Starters

The sharing of meals is the essence of the Greek kitchen; family and friends gathered together, a neighbour who just dropped in to say `hello' and ends up staying for a while... chatting, having an ouzo, breaking a piece of bread from the loaf on the table.

And, of course, some meze, whether small plates of feta cheese and olives drizzled with glorious olive oil and sprinkled with fragrant oregano, or something more substantial, such as keftethes. Bread accompanies all meals; it is essential at the Greek table. These delicious small plates of food can, at times, become a complete meal.

These delicious fried meatballs are perfect on a meze platter as a starter accompanied with tzatziki, feta cheese, roasted red capsicum or your own mix of nibbles. No Greek celebration goes by without keftethes.

Keftethes
meatballs

2 thick slices of day-old bread, crusts removed
450 g (1 lb) minced (ground) beef
2 eggs
1 onion, finely chopped or grated
60 g (2 oz/ ¼ cup) chopped parsley
1 tablespoon dried oregano
salt and pepper, to taste
plain (all-purpose) flour, for coating
olive oil, for frying

Soak the bread in a shallow plate of water, squeeze out the excess and crumble the bread. Mix well in a bowl with the other ingredients; the mixture should be moist. Refrigerate for about 1 hour.

Take small pieces of the meat mixture and roll into walnut-sized balls. Sift a little flour on a plate and roll the balls in it to coat them all over. Heat the olive oil in a frying pan over medium heat. Add the meatballs a few at a time and turn regularly to brown on all sides. Continue to cook until cooked through. Serve hot or at room temperature.

My mother always liked to grate her onions using a hand held grater instead of chopping and dicing them. This is something I also noticed many women doing in Greece. She did this for her keftethes and most of her casseroles.

Keftethes
in tomato sauce

Tomato sauce

75ml (2½ fl oz, ⅓ cup) olive
oil
1 onion, finely chopped
2 garlic cloves, finely chopped
2 x 400 g (14 oz) cans diced
tomatoes
1 teaspoon sugar
2 tablespoons chopped parsley
salt and pepper, to taste
Meatballs

In a heavy pan, heat the olive oil over medium heat and
sauté the onions and garlic until soft. Add the remaining
ingredients and season to taste.

Add the meatballs and continue to cook for 5 minutes
on the stove top. Serve hot with potatoes or rice and a
green salad.

You can also use the tomato sauce with pasta, fried
potatoes, fried zucchini (courgette) or eggplant
(aubergine).

Feta is a staple food in Greece. It adds flavour and texture to all foods. Roasted, it tastes delicious smeared on crusty bread.

Roasted feta

400 g (14 oz) feta cheese, sliced
black pepper
olive oil
1 teaspoon dried oregano
lemon wedges

Preheat the oven to 200°C (400°F/Gas mark 6).

Arrange aluminium foil on a baking tray and put slices of feta cheese on it. Season with pepper. Drizzle oil over then sprinkle oregano on top. Fold the foil over the cheese and bake for 10 minutes.

Open the foil carefully and squeeze lemon juice over the cheese. Serve while hot.

Taramasalata is one of the best-known traditional Greek dips. When you buy the roe from your fishmonger it will be a dark red colour, which lightens to pale pink as you whisk your ingredients together.

Taramasalata
fish roe dip

6 slices day-old white bread, crusts removed
240 g (8½ oz) salted fish roe
2 tablespoons onion, finely diced
250 ml (8 fl oz, 1 cup) olive oil
60 ml (2 fl oz, ¼ cup) lemon juice

Soak the bread in a shallow bowl of water, squeeze out the excess and crumble the bread.

Using a large mortar and pestle, pound the fish roe into a paste. Add the onion, a few drops of oil and keep beating. Add a small amount of bread, along with the rest of the oil and lemon juice. Continue adding bread, a little at a time, beating continuously until all is combined. Adding these ingredients slowly will prevent curdling and create a thick pale pink dip.

Serve with fresh crusty bread.

You can use a food processor if you don't have a mortar and pestle. Add ingredients slowly.

Two cooked, medium-sized potatoes can be used instead of, or in combination with, the bread.

I love this dip. It's one of my favourites on a meze platter with some crusty bread. It takes a little time to bake the eggplant, but it's worth it when you have the smoky aroma.

Melitzanosalata
eggplant dip

1 kg (2¼ lb) eggplant (aubergine)
pinch of salt
3 garlic cloves, crushed
125 ml (4 fl oz, ½ cup) olive oil
60 ml (2 fl oz, ¼ cup) white wine vinegar (use lemon juice, if you prefer)
2 tablespoons chopped parsley

Preheat the oven to 200°C (400°F/Gas mark 6).

Bake the eggplants whole for about 40 minutes or until tender. Run under cold water and peel immediately while still hot. Chop the eggplants, then put in a bowl and season with salt and garlic. Continue to mash the flesh using a fork.

Add the oil, a little at a time, alternating with the vinegar until all is used up. Fold in the parsley and place in a serving dish. Cover and refrigerate to chill.

Serve with fresh crusty bread.

This is sensational with lamb and goes very well on a meze platter with keftethes and pita bread. I particularly love this dip with cheese triangles or fried zucchini as a light lunch on a hot summer's day.

Tzatziki
cucumber and yogurt dip

675 g (1½ lb) plain Greek yogurt
1 cucumber, peeled, seeded and chopped
4 garlic cloves, crushed
1 tablespoon olive oil
3 tablespoons dill, finely chopped
squeeze of lemon
pinch of salt

Drain the yogurt in a sieve lined with absorbent paper or muslin for about 1 hour. Discard the liquid.

Place the yogurt into a bowl and add all the other ingredients. Season to taste. Cover and refrigerate until needed.

Serve with pita or fresh crusty bread.

Garlic dip is the perfect accompaniment to fish or meatballs. If you are just in the mood for some garlic, spread some onto pita bread and enjoy.

Skordalia
garlic dip

450 g (1 lb) potatoes
6 garlic cloves, crushed
475 ml (16 fl oz) olive oil
juice of 1 lemon
2 tablespoons white wine vinegar
salt and pepper, to taste

Cook the potatoes in a large pan of salted boiling water. When cooked, drain and peel while hot.

Using a mortar and pestle or food processor, mash the potatoes to a purée. Add the garlic, olive oil, lemon juice and vinegar in turns, while you beat continuously. Add a little hot water if it gets too thick.

Skordalia with walnuts

75 g (2½ oz) walnuts,
shelled and finely chopped
2 egg yolks
Skordalia Dip

Add walnuts to skordalia together with two egg yolks, combining all ingredients well.

Since my family loves feta and roasted red capsicum, I make a large batch of this dish. It keeps in the refrigerator for a few days, if it lasts that long! Prepared peppers in jars will do the job beautifully too.

Htipiti

feta and capsicum dip

115 g (4 oz) red onions, peeled
75 ml (2½ fl oz) olive oil
330 g (11½ oz) roasted red capsicum (bell peppers)
280 g (10 oz) feta cheese
2 tablespoons chopped parsley
salt and pepper, to taste

Preheat the oven to 200°C (400°F/Gas mark 6).

Put the onions on a baking sheet, drizzled with a little of the olive oil, and roast for about 30 minutes, or until soft.

Chop the capsicum and onions finely and mash together with the feta cheese. Add the remaining oil and parsley and mix well. Season to taste.

Serve with fresh crusty bread.

My father would often visit just for a coffee and end up staying a while. If I didn't have a meal prepared this is what he would always ask for: simple but delicious.

Greek-style scrambled eggs

200 g (7 oz) feta cheese
3–4 eggs
black pepper, to taste

Heat a little oil in a large frying pan over medium heat. Crumble the feta into the pan and add the eggs. Mix well and season with a little black pepper.

You could add some chopped tomato into the egg and cheese mixture, if you like. Stir until scrambled to the desired texture.

Serve with fresh crusty bread, or do as my father did and make sandwiches with it.

This is one of my father's favourite snacks. There were many times he would make a meal out of it by adding black olives and fresh bread — and, of course, a glass of ouzo.

Pan-fried feta

vegetable oil, for frying
250 g (9 oz) feta cheese, cubed
plain (all-purpose) flour, for coating
lemon juice, to drizzling

Heat the oil in a large frying pan.
Dust the cheese with flour and fry until golden and crispy. Serve immediately. I like it with a squeeze of lemon.

Traditionally the cheese used for saganaki is the Greek kefalotiri, however, you can use haloumi if you prefer. This is a quick, simple and very tasty meze.

Saganaki

250 g (9 oz) kefalotiri cheese
plain (all-purpose) flour, for dusting
olive oil, for frying
lemon juice, for drizzling

Cut the cheese into slices about 1 cm (½ in) thick and dust with a little flour.

Heat about 2 tablespoons of oil in a frying pan and fry the cheese until golden and crispy, turning once only.

When cooked, place onto a platter or leave in the pan. Squeeze on some lemon juice and serve immediately.

It is a cold autumn afternoon, the heating is on, leaves are covering the driveway and pastitso is the meal of the evening. While making the meat sauce and cooking the pasta for the pastitso I am sorting out olives that a kind friend has given me from her olive tree. This is my first time pickling olives so I have been on the phone to aunts and friends for some ideas on how to prepare them.

My youngest daughter is home from school so she is given the task of sorting and scoring olives while I put the pastitso together. My favourite CD is on and life can't get much better than this. Hope the olives turn out okay. I can hear the front door... the rest of the family is arriving, one at a time. The house is filled once again with chatter and laughter and discussions about everyone's day.

Preserved olives

Scored olives
salt

Place your scored olives – scoring helps in the preserving and drawing out the bitterness – in a large basin or bucket and cover with cold clean water. I used a large plastic basin for this and I place a large plate on the olives so they stayed submerged in the water. Change the water daily.

After 3 or 4 days, start adding salt to the water. I add 225 g (8 oz, 1 cup) coarse salt to 2.4 litres (4 pints, 10 cups) of water. Again cover with a plate so that all the olives are under the salty water. Pour out this liquid and replace with clean salty water daily for about 2 weeks. You will know when your olives are ready simply by tasting them to see if the bitterness has gone.

When the olives are ready to be bottled, pour them into clean, sterilised jars and prepare the brine. Again, use a ratio of 225 g (8 oz, 1 cup) of salt to 2.4 litres (4 pints, 10 cups) of water. Bring this mixture to the boil, allow to cool and then carefully pour over the olives, covering them completely. Pour a little olive oil on top to seal and put lids

on. Store in a cool cupboard until they are ready for use, about 6 months. They should keep for about 12 months.

When you are ready to use your olives, pour out the salty brine, replace with clean fresh water and refrigerate. There should be enough salt in the olives to seep out into the water and create a weak salty brine. You can add some garlic, oregano and lemon juice at this stage, if you like, or any other preferred flavourings.

I leave the olives in this weak brine until I want to use them. Then I take out some olives and cover them with some oil, a little fresh lemon juice or vinegar, garlic, black pepper and oregano and let them soak overnight... delicious.

Roasted capsicums are delicious on a meze platter or just as a light meal for one. When my mother was short of time she would simply chop the capsicums up into pieces and fry them in olive oil, adding salt and garlic at the end.

Roasted
red capsicums

6 large red capsicums (bell peppers)
salt
olive oil
white wine vinegar
2–3 garlic cloves, crushed (optional)

Preheat the oven to 200°C (400°F/Gas mark 6).

Wash the capsicums and place on a baking sheet. Bake until the skins have blistered, turning once only during baking. Remove from the oven and allow to cool. Peel to remove and discard the skins, then cut the flesh into pieces and arrange on a plate.

Season with salt, a drizzle of olive oil and some white wine vinegar. Add garlic, if you like.

Serve warm or cold; they taste even better the next day.

These fried zucchini are quick and easy to make and are often served as a meze with tzatziki or skordalia. You can also use eggplant and prepare them the same way.

Fried zucchini

4 zucchini (courgettes)
plain (all-purpose) flour, for coating
olive oil, for frying
salt, to taste

Wash and slice the zucchini lengthways. Coat in plain flour and fry in olive oil.

Drain onto a plate with some absorbent paper and season to taste.

Serve with tzatziki and pita bread.

For a light lunch on a hot summer's day these rissoles are beautiful served with a salad. You can also serve them as a meze, or as a side to a meat dish.

Vegetable rissoles

450 g (1 lb) zucchini
(courgettes)
1 onion, finely diced
1 garlic clove, finely diced
(optional)
2 eggs, lightly beaten
150 g (5 oz) feta cheese,
crumbled
1 tablespoon oregano
salt and pepper, to taste
2-3 slices bread, crusts
removed
plain (all-purpose) flour, for
dusting
olive oil

Wash and dry the zucchini and grate (shred) into a large bowl. Squeeze out and discard the excess juice.

Add the onion, garlic, beaten eggs, crumbled feta cheese and oregano. Season with salt and pepper.

Crumble the bread in a food processor and add to mixture. Mix well with your hands. Roll into small balls and press into rissole shapes. Roll in flour to coat lightly.

Heat the olive oil in a large frying pan and cook the rissoles until golden and crispy. Place on kitchen paper to absorb the excess oil and serve with a squeeze of lemon.

Greek-style scrambled eggs makes a perfect light lunch, especially on a hot summer's day when tomatoes are at their best: sweet and delicious.

Scrambled eggs with tomatoes

6 medium tomatoes
3 tablespoons olive oil
salt and pepper, to taste
½ teaspoon sugar
1 teaspoon oregano
8 eggs, beaten
2 spring onions (scallions),
sliced

Wash the tomatoes and chop into dice.

In a large frying pan, heat the olive oil, add the tomatoes and stir well. Season to taste, add the sugar and oregano and cook over medium heat for about 7–10 minutes.

Pour the eggs slowly into the tomato mixture, stirring until the eggs are cooked.

Serve warm garnished with spring onions.

This recipe uses capsicums that are simply roasted, peeled and chopped without any dressing or seasonings.

Scrambled eggs with roasted red capsicum

8 eggs, beaten
4 tomatoes, diced
4 roasted red capsicums (bell peppers), chopped
125 g (4 oz, ½ cup) feta cheese, crumbled
1 teaspoon oregano
salt and pepper, to taste
25 g (1 oz) butter
1 tablespoon chopped parsley

Place the eggs in a large bowl and beat them lightly. Add the tomatoes, roasted red peppers, feta cheese, oregano, salt and pepper and combine.

Melt the butter in a large frying pan over medium heat and pour in the egg mixture, stirring until the eggs are cooked through. Garnish with parsley and serve immediately.

Delicious on their own as a meze or as a side to grilled meats, these patatokeftethes are lovely. I particularly love the flavours of the garlic and Parmesan; not traditionally Greek but it seems to work.

Patatokeftethes
potato croquettes

900 g (2 lb) potatoes
2 eggs
115 g (4 oz, ½ cup) Parmesan, grated (shredded)
1 small onion, finely chopped
1 teaspoon oregano
1 tablespoon chopped parsley
2 garlic cloves, finely chopped
salt and pepper, to taste
plain (all-purpose) flour, for dusting
oil, for frying

Cook the unpeeled potatoes in a large pan of boiling water for about 20–30 minutes, or until soft. Drain, then peel when cool.

Place the potatoes into a large bowl and mash well. Add the eggs, Parmesan, onion, oregano, parsley and garlic. Season with salt and pepper.

Using your hands, mix all the ingredients well and shape into small rissoles. Dust the rissoles in a little flour, until lightly coated all over.

Heat some oil in a large frying pan and fry the rissoles in small batches until golden brown and crispy, turning once.

Feta cheese is the typical Greek table cheese. It is usually made with sheeps' or goats' milk. It's a beautiful white cheese that is a little salty and soft, yet firm enough to crumble or cut into pieces. Feta is probably best known as a main ingredient in Greek salad. My mother would buy her cheese monthly — it was packaged in large cans and stored in brine.

Feta cheese was one of my father's favourite foods. He could have it for breakfast, lunch or dinner. When a friend would drop in, there would always be a small plate with cubes of feta drizzled with olive oil and sprinkled with oregano to nibble on while discussing life and politics over a glass of ouzo.

These are the memories that have woven their way into my mind... these are the things that I love.

Soups

Soups are very popular in Greece, especially in winter. However, I also like to make these wholesome soups all year round.

If you were to choose a classic Greek soup that every household would make, it would be bean soup. Some would even say that it is the national dish of Greece. Simple, healthy and declicious.

There are also soups for special occasions. Mayeritsa is eaten at Easter time only, breaking the fasting period.

My family's favourite is the comforting chicken soup known as avgolemeno.

The egg and lemon sauce used to finish this soup is popular in Greek cooking. This soup is not only simple but nourishing and delicious also. Perfect for a Sunday night dinner.

Yiouverlakia soup
meatball soup with egg and lemon sauce

450 g (1 lb) minced (ground) beef
1 small onion, finely diced
75 g (2½ oz, ⅓ cup) short-grain rice
2 tablespoons chopped parsley, plus extra to garnish
1 tablespoon finely chopped mint or dill
salt and pepper, to taste
50 g (1¾ oz) butter
Egg and Lemon Sauce (see Dressings and Sauces)

In a large bowl, combine the mince, onion, half the rice, herbs and seasonings. Shape this mixture into small balls.

Pour 1.2 litres (2 pints, 5 cups) water into a large pan and add the butter. Bring to the boil. Slowly add the meatballs to the boiling water, together with the remaining rice. Cook for approximately 20 minutes, or until cooked.

Make the Egg and Lemon Sauce and add to the soup.

Season to taste, garnish with a sprig of parsley, if you wish, and serve hot.

My mother made this soup almost every Friday, and the Fridays that she didn't she would make lentil soup. It was almost a ritual.

Fasolada
Greek bean soup

450 g (1 lb) dried cannellini (white) beans
1 onion, finely diced
olive oil
2 small carrots, peeled and sliced
2 stalks celery, sliced
1 x 400 g (14 oz) can diced tomatoes
2 bay leaves
salt and pepper, to taste

Soak the beans in cold water overnight. The next day drain them, then set aside.

In a large pan, sauté the onion in a little olive oil. Add the sliced carrots, celery, tomatoes and bay leaves. Pour in about 1 litre (1¾ pints) of water and the drained beans. Bring to the boil and simmer for about 1 hour, or until the beans are cooked. Add more water if needed. Season to taste.

Serve hot accompanied with crusty bread, feta cheese, olives and pickled vegetables.

This chicken soup is the most typical of Greek cooking. It stirs childhood memories, and I now make it for my family regularly, especially if someone isn't feeling well. It seems to cure everything.

Chicken soup avgolemeno

1 whole chicken
250 g (9 oz) fine noodles (angel hair)
salt and pepper, to taste
Egg and Lemon Sauce (see Dressings and Sauces)

Wash the chicken and place it in a large pan with enough water to cover. Bring to the boil and cook until tender, skimming off the scum as it rises to the surface. Remove the chicken and strain the stock.

Bring the stock back to the boil, add the noodles and simmer until cooked. Season to taste.

Make the Egg and Lemon Sauce and add to the soup.

Serve the soup hot accompanied with the chicken meat, which can be either hot or cold.

You can substitute the noodles with 100 g (3½ oz/ ½ cup) short- or medium-grain rice.

A steaming bowl of lentil soup is just the thing to sustain you through cold winter days. It makes a perfect lunch dish. Make it in batches and freeze in portions, if you like.

Lentil soup

450 g (1 lb) lentils
1 onion, finely diced
2 garlic cloves, finely chopped
olive oil
1 x 400 g (14 oz) can diced tomatoes
2 bay leaves
pinch of oregano
salt and pepper, to taste
1 tablespoon vinegar

Wash the lentils and drain in a colander.

Sauté the onions and garlic in a little olive oil in a large pot. Add the drained lentils, tomatoes, bay leaves and oregano. Pour in 1 litre (1¾ pints) of water and bring to the boil. Simmer until the lentils are cooked.

Season to taste and pour in the vinegar at the end.

Serve hot accompanied with feta cheese, olives, pickled vegetables and fresh bread.

You can also add diced carrots and celery to this soup, if you like.

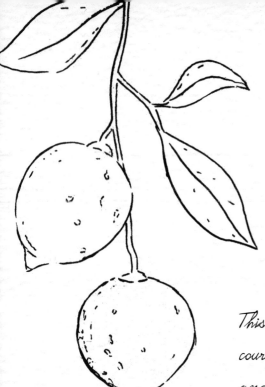

This rich and delicious fish soup gives you two courses, the soup and then the wonderful fish and vegetables. I like to serve everything at the same time, together with fresh crusty bread.

Fish soup avgolemono

1 small onion, peeled and quartered
2 carrots, scrubbed and halved
2 celery stalks, chopped into quarters
2 large potatoes, peeled and cut into chunks
10 peppercorns
salt
1.3 kg (3 lb) fish (I like to use snapper)
olive oil
lemon juice
75 g (2½ oz, ⅓ cup) short- or medium-grain rice
Egg and Lemon Sauce (see Dressings and Sauces)
salt and pepper, to taste
white pepper, to garnish

Put the vegetables and peppercorns in a large pan of salted boiling water and bring to the boil.

While they are cooking, wash and clean the fish. If the fish is large, cut it in half and place into the boiling water with the vegetables. Simmer for about 15 minutes, or until the fish is cooked.

Remove the fish and vegetables carefully with a slotted spoon and set aside. Place the vegetables on a platter. Remove the flesh from the fish and arrange on the platter with the vegetables. Drizzle over some olive oil and lemon juice.

Sieve the stock through muslin or absorbent paper into a clean pan and bring to the boil. Add the rice and simmer until cooked.

Add the Egg and Lemon Sauce and season to taste.

Garnish with white pepper. Serve hot accompanied by the fish and vegetables.

This light and healthy soup is lovely with feta cheese, olives and fresh bread.

Revithada

chickpea soup

450 g (1 lb) dried chickpeas
1 large onion, finely chopped
3 tablespoons olive oil, plus
extra to drizzle
salt and pepper
⅓ cup parsley, chopped
1 lemon

Soak the chickpeas in cold water overnight.

In a large pan, sauté the onion in olive oil until soft.

Drain the chickpeas and rinse them under cold water. Tip into the pan with the onions and mix well, coating them in the oil.

Add enough cold water to cover the chickpeas and then add a little extra. Bring to the boil, removing any scum that comes to the surface. Simmer for about 1–1½ hours, or until the chickpeas are soft and tender. To thicken the soup a little, remove about a cupful of chickpeas and mash them using a fork. Return to the soup and stir well. You can mash more chickpeas if you like your soup thicker.

Season with salt and pepper and stir in the parsley. Serve with a drizzle of olive oil and a squeeze of lemon juice. It's also perfect with some pickled vegetables, olives and fresh bread.

Beautiful, classic blue and white images come to mind when thinking of the Greek islands. White-washed walls, cobblestone paths, blue windows and doors, and dome-shaped churches where you're always welcome to enter, light a candle and spend a few quiet moments.

The charming villages on these islands are breathtaking. Rows of houses coloured pink and yellow, clotheslines draped with washing, open windows with pots of flowers sitting on the windowsill atop a lace doily. Warm and friendly.

Main Meals

I love the meals that you can make in one pot and let simmer, or roast simply prepared in the oven to bake to perfection, filling the house with appetising scents.

Lamb is always a favourite in Greece, whether it is oven-roasted or cooked on a spit, marinated simply with olive oil, salt, pepper, oregano and, of course, freshly squeezed lemon juice - tempting and delicious.

My family's favourite, apart from succulent roast lamb, is yemista. I also love making this dish; yemista can be prepared earlier in the day and served when needed. I particularly love the fragrant aroma of red capsicum baking in my kitchen.

This is a favourite in my house. I love the aroma of the red peppers cooking in the oven and their glorious red colour. I also love that it can be made in advance and served either warm or at room temperature.

Yemista
stuffed red peppers

8 medium red capsicums (bell peppers)
1 onion, finely chopped
olive oil
675 g (1½ lb) minced (ground) beef
680 ml (22 fl oz) tomato passata
450 g (1 lb) medium-grain rice
parsley, chopped
salt and pepper, to taste

Preheat the oven to 200°C (400°F/Gas mark 6).

Wash the capsicums and slice off the tops. Set aside.

In a large frying pan, sauté the onions in a little olive oil until soft. Add the mince and tomato passata and mix well. Add 300 ml (½ pint) water, rice, parsley and season with salt and pepper. Cook for about 5–10 minutes.

Spoon the mixture into the peppers, put the tops back on and place in a large baking dish. Drizzle a little olive oil over them and place in the oven for about 1 hour, or until cooked. You may need a little water in the base of the dish.

Serve with a green salad, feta cheese and fresh bread.

My family loves pastitso. I like to serve it with a lovely Greek salad and some feta cheese. I think the feta goes so well with this dish that I now add it in the pastitso as well.

Pastitso

675 g (1½ lb) rigatoni
1 tablespoon butter
salt
1 onion, finely chopped
1 garlic clove, finely chopped
olive oil
675 g (1½ lb) minced
(ground) beef
680 ml (22 fl oz) tomato
passata
100 ml (3½ fl oz) red wine
salt and pepper, to taste
1 bay leaf
1 teaspoon oregano
100 g (3½ oz) feta cheese
Béchamel Sauce (see
Dressings and Sauces)

Preheat the oven to 200°C (400°F/Gas mark 6).

Cook the pasta in a large pan of water. When cooked, drain, then toss in the butter and season with a little salt.

Sauté the onions and garlic in a large saucepan with a little olive oil. Add the mince and cook until browned. Add the tomato passata and 300 ml (½ pint) water. Mix well and add a splash of red wine. Season to taste. Add the oregano and bay leaf. Cook for about 20 minutes, or until almost cooked.

Meanwhile, prepare the béchamel sauce and set aside.

In a large baking dish, place half the pasta, top with mince mixture and crumble the feta cheese over. Top with the remaining pasta and then the béchamel sauce. Bake for 45 minutes or until golden brown.

Serve with Greek salad.

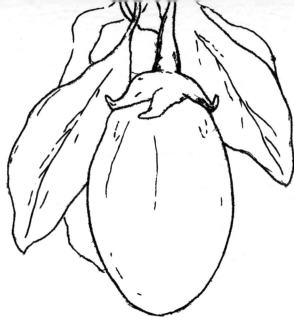

This may seem labour intensive — and it is —
but you can fry the eggplant and potatoes earlier
in the day, or prepare the mince sauce ahead of
time. Putting everything together can be fun.

Moussaka

4 large eggplants
(aubergines), sliced
salt
4 large potatoes, peeled and
sliced
olive oil
1 large onion, finely diced
2 garlic cloves, finely diced
675 g (1½ lb) minced beef
680 ml (22 fl oz) tomato
passata
1 bay leaf
1 teaspoon oregano
salt and pepper, to taste
Béchamel Sauce (see
Dressings and Sauces)
100 g (3½ oz) feta cheese

Preheat the oven to 200°C (400°F/Gas mark 6).

Sprinkle the eggplant with salt and leave to drain in a colander for ½ an hour. Rinse and pat dry with kitchen paper.

Put the sliced potatoes in a bowl of water so they don't discolour.

Heat a little olive oil in a frying pan and fry the potatoes until golden brown. Place on some kitchen paper to absorb any excess oil when cooked. Fry the eggplant, using the same frying pan with any remaining oil. They may need a little more attention as they will tend to absorb more oil than the potatoes.

In a heavy saucepan, heat some oil and sauté the onions and garlic until soft. Add the beef and stir until brown. Add the tomato passata, 250 ml (8 fl oz, 1 cup) of water, the bay leaf, oregano and seasoning to taste.

Prepare the béchamel sauce.

Pour a little olive oil into a baking dish to grease it and arrange the eggplant slices on top. Top with a layer of potatoes. Pour the meat mixture on top and crumble over the feta cheese. Arrange the remaining eggplant and potatoes.

Pour the prepared sauce on top of the vegetables and bake for about 45 minutes, or until golden.

Serve with a green salad.

See picture next page.

I love this charming meal. I used to love helping my mother make the dolmades. As they are a little fiddly, it is nice to have someone to share the job.

Dolmades
stuffed cabbage leaves

1 large cabbage
675 g (1½ lb) minced
(ground) beef
1 onion, finely chopped
300 g (11 oz) medium-grain
rice,
75 g (2½ oz, ⅓ cup) parsley,
finely chopped
salt and pepper, to taste
1 tablespoon tomato paste
1 tablespoon olive oil, plus
extra to drizzle
Egg and Lemon Sauce (see
Dressings and Sauces)

Wash the cabbage well. Carefully cut into the core with a sharp knife and remove it. Place the cabbage into a large saucepan filled with water and bring to the boil. Simmer for 15 minutes. Remove carefully, drain and allow to cool.

When cool enough to touch, start removing cabbage leaves, one at a time, and set aside. You can put the cabbage back into hot water if it becomes difficult to detach the leaves. Trim the hard stems of the leaves and cut into 2, or into pieces large enough to roll.

In a large bowl, combine the meat, onion, rice, parsley, seasonings, tomato paste and oil.

Line a large casserole dish with 2 or 3 cabbage leaves.

Place a cabbage leaf into the palm of your hand and place 1 tablespoon of the meat mixture in the leaf. Fold the leaf base over it, turn the sides in and roll up. Place in the casserole dish, seam side down. Repeat until all the mixture is used. You may have more than one layer of cabbage rolls; make sure they are packed tightly.

Pour 250 ml (8 fl oz, 1 cup) hot water over and drizzle some olive oil on top.

Place a heavy plate upside down over the rolls to keep them in shape. Simmer for about 45 minutes, or until cooked.

When cool, pour over the sauce.

This dish was one of my mother's favourites. She loved the unusual flavours of the lamb and lettuce with the egg and lemon sauce. She always served it with fresh bread and savoured every last drop of the sauce.

Lamb and lettuce fricassée

1 onion, finely chopped
6 spring onions (scallions), sliced
olive oil
900 g (2 lb) leg of lamb, boned and cut into chunks
2 cos or iceberg lettuce, roughly chopped
large handful dill, finely chopped
salt and pepper, to taste
Egg and Lemon Sauce (see Dressings and Sauces)

Sauté the onion and spring onion in a large saucepan with a little olive oil.

Add the meat and cook for about 5 minutes until browned on all sides.

Pour in enough water to cover the meat, bring to the boil and simmer for about 1 hour, or until tender. Add the roughly chopped lettuce and dill, season to taste and continue cooking for another 15 minutes. Remove from the heat and allow to rest.

Make the egg and lemon sauce and add to the casserole. Shake the pan a little to combine the sauce with the juices.

Serve warm with crusty fresh bread.

This flavourful and tender lamb roast is a real favourite in my family. The meat falls off the bone and melts in your mouth. I particularly love the tangy lemon taste.

Classic Greek lamb

1.8 kg (4 lb) leg of lamb
salt and pepper
dried oregano
4 garlic cloves, crushed
olive oil
juice of 1 lemon

Preheat the oven to 160°C–180°C (325°F–350°F/ Gas mark 3–4).

Place the meat in a roasting pan and season with salt, pepper, oregano and garlic. Drizzle some olive oil onto the meat and pour lemon juice on top.

Pour 125 ml (4 fl oz, ½ cup) of water into the pan and cover with a lid or foil. Place into the oven and cook slowly for 3 hours. Turn the meat while cooking, basting with pan juices and adding more water if it gets too dry. Turn the temperature down to 140°C–160°C (275°F–325°F/Gas mark 2–3) and cook for another 1–1½ hours.

When cooked, the meat should fall off the bone. Serve with lemon potatoes and a Greek salad.

Lemon and oregano potatoes

1.8 kg (4 lb) potatoes
juice of 1 lemon
75 ml (2½ fl oz, ⅓ cup) olive oil
salt and pepper
oregano

Preheat the oven to 200°C (400°F/Gas mark 6).

Wash and peel the potatoes. Cut into quarters and combine with lemon juice, olive oil, salt, pepper and oregano. Transfer to a baking dish and bake for about 45 minutes, or until cooked (depending on the size of the potatoes). I sometimes add a little water to the baking dish.

Serve with roast meats.

This is a gorgeous, sweet-tasting casserole, especially delicious if you have sweet, fresh tomatoes. You can omit the lamb for a light vegetarian meal served simply with fresh crusty bread. I also love it with some feta cheese.

Lamb and okra casserole

1 large onion, finely diced
olive oil
1.8 kg (4 lb) lamb shoulder, diced
680 ml (22 fl oz) tomato passata (or 6 fresh tomatoes, chopped)
salt and pepper, to taste
450 g (1 lb) jar okra

In a large casserole dish, sauté the onions in olive oil until soft. Add the meat and sauté until brown.

Add the tomato passata and 500 ml (16 fl oz, 2 cups) of water, or enough to cover the meat. Season with salt and pepper. Cover and simmer until the meat is tender.

Meanwhile, drain and rinse the okra. Add to the meat and continue cooking until both meat and okra are tender. As the okra are delicate, do not stir while cooking, just shake the dish and add more water if needed. The okra will probably only need to be cooked for 15 minutes.

Serve with fresh bread.

If my husband was to choose his favourite Greek meal this would be the one. It is a one-pot, simple but enticing meal, served with some fresh crusty bread.

Pork and celery avgolemono

olive oil
1 small onion, finely chopped
1.3 kg (3 lb) pork shoulder, cut into pieces (if you prefer you can use pork cutlets)
salt and pepper to taste
1 large bunch celery
Egg and Lemon Sauce (see Dressings and Sauces)
ground black pepper

Heat the oil in a large casserole dish and sauté the onion and meat until slightly brown.

Pour in 500 ml (16 fl oz, 2 cups) of water, season and cover. Simmer for about ½ hour, or until the meat is tender.

Meanwhile, wash and trim the celery and cut into 4 cm (1¾ in) pieces. Add to the meat and cook until the celery is soft; do not overcook.

Prepare the egg and lemon sauce and pour into the casserole. Allow to rest for 5–10 minutes, then serve with some ground black pepper.

This is a hearty and delicious meal. It is so simple, yet perfect for a cold winter's day served with fresh crusty bread.

Pork with leeks

3–4 large leeks
olive oil
1 small onion, finely diced
1.3 kg (3 lb) pork shoulder or
leg, cut into chunks
500 ml (16 fl oz, 2 cups)
tomato passata
salt and pepper
1 teaspoon sweet paprika
(optional)
ground black pepper, to taste

Wash and trim the leeks well and cut into 4 cm (1¾ in) pieces. Set aside.

Heat the oil in a large casserole dish and sauté the onions and meat until brown. Add the tomato passata and season to taste. Pour in 500 ml (16 fl oz/2 cups) of water, cover and cook until the pork is almost cooked. Add the leeks and continue simmering until the meat and leeks are tender. Add more water if it looks too dry.

Serve hot, seasoned with ground pepper. Serve with feta cheese and fresh crusty bread.

I like to use a whole snapper for this dish but you can use any firm white fish fillets. I like to add potatoes to this dish rather than serve them separately, the potatoes absorbing the wonderful tomato sauce.

Baked fish

4 large onions, sliced
2 garlic cloves, finely chopped
olive oil
6 fresh tomatoes, chopped
handful of finely chopped
parsley
salt and pepper, to taste
1.3 kg (3 lb) firm white fish
fillets
lemon slices

Preheat the oven to 200°C (400°F/Gas mark 6).

Sauté the onions and garlic in a large baking dish with a little olive oil. Add the chopped tomatoes and parsley and season to taste. Add 125 ml (4 fl oz, ½ cup) water and combine well. Place the cleaned fish on the tomato mixture and cover with some of the sauce. Bake for 30–40 minutes, or until the fish is cooked.

Serve hot with potatoes and a green salad.

I love these delicate, lemony, oregano-flavoured lamb cutlets. Nothing can be more perfect on warm summer nights, served with tzatziki and a glorious big Greek salad.

Grilled lamb cutlets

12 lamb cutlets
60 ml (2 fl oz, ¼ cup) olive oil
3 tablespoons lemon juice
oregano
salt and pepper, to taste

Marinate the lamb cutlets in the oil, lemon juice and oregano for at least 2 hours.

Grill (broil) for about 15 minutes, or until cooked to your taste, turning once, and season with salt and pepper.

Serve hot with tzatziki, potatoes and salad.

Braised cauliflower with tomato and smoked sweet paprika

1 small brown onion, diced
olive oil
1 medium cauliflower, cut into florets
2 large ripe tomatoes, diced
1 teaspoon smoked sweet paprika
salt and pepper, to taste
flat-leafed parsley, finely chopped, to garnish

Sauté the onion in a large pan with a little olive oil. Add the cauliflower and brown a little.

Put the tomato on the cauliflower and add enough water to cover. Add the smoked sweet paprika and season to taste. You can add more or less paprika, depending on how much heat you like. Cover and cook until the cauliflower is just tender. Garnish with parsley.

Serve with fresh crusty bread or as a side to fish or meat dishes.

I prefer to shake the pan from side to side when I check the cauliflower during the cooking process, rather than stirring, so I don't break the florets.

Roast pork is a favourite in my family and is really very simple to prepare. You can also use a pork loin rack, if you prefer.

Greek roast pork

1.3 kg (3 lb) leg of pork
salt and pepper, to taste
1 tablespoon dried rosemary
juice of 1 lemon
juice of 1 orange
5 garlic cloves, halved

Preheat the oven to 200°C (400°F/Gas mark 6).

Prepare the meat by washing and patting dry with some kitchen paper. Using a sharp knife, score the top into diamond shapes.

Place the pork onto a roasting pan and rub salt, pepper, rosemary, lemon and orange juice all over the meat. Tuck the garlic into the skin where you have scored it.

Bake for about 1½ hours. I pour 250 ml (8 fl oz/ 1 cup) juice into the baking dish. The meat won't need turning but baste it with the juices in the pan occasionally, adding more water if you think it is getting too dry.

Turn the oven to 220°C (425°F/Gas mark 7) for the last 20 minutes so that the pork crisps to a glorious golden colour.

Serve hot with roast potatoes and salad.

My mother would grate the tomatoes for this dish. She would cut them in half, hold half of the tomato in the palm of her hand and grate the flesh into a bowl. The skin was the only thing left in her hand.

Roast potatoes with tomato

8 large potatoes
olive oil
50 g (1¾ oz) butter or margarine
6 fresh tomatoes, diced
salt and pepper, to taste
oregano
sweet paprika (optional)

Preheat the oven to 200°C (400°F/Gas mark 6).

Peel the potatoes and chop into chunks or wedges. Place into a large baking dish, drizzle with some olive oil and dot with butter. Pour over the tomatoes and season with salt, pepper, oregano and paprika.

Cover with aluminium foil and bake for approximately 30 minutes. Remove the foil and bake for another 30 minutes, or until the potatoes are tender and the sauce has thickened a little. Keep on eye on the potatoes while cooking so they don't dry up. Add a little water if needed.

This is best served hot and perfect with roast meats.

Make sure that you cook the meat thoroughly in this dish as it must be soft before adding the pasta. You can add as much or as little of the feta as you like, or leave it to each member of your family to add their own.

Lamb and macaroni casserole

1 large onion, finely diced
olive oil
2 stalks celery, finely chopped
2 garlic cloves, finely diced
2 carrots, peeled and sliced
2 bay leaves
1 teaspoon dried oregano
1.8 kg (4 lb) lamb shoulder, cut into cubes
680 ml (22 fl oz) tomato passata
450 g (1 lb) pasta shells
parsley
salt and pepper, to taste
200 g (7 oz) feta cheese

Sauté the onion in a large casserole dish with a little olive oil. Add the celery, garlic, carrots, bay leaves and oregano and mix well. Add the lamb chunks and brown the mean. Add tomato passata and 1 litre (1¾ pints. 4 cups) water, ensuring that the meat is covered. Bring to the boil and cook until the lamb is soft and tender.

Add the pasta (topping up water, if requried) and cook until tender. Season to taste.

Serve with chopped parsley and crumbled feta.

This tastes even better the next day.

This is a dish that I make regularly. I always make enough of the chicken stock to make the chicken avgolemono soup too. I love that I can have two courses from this chicken dish: simple, delicious and wholesome.

Oven-baked chicken and rice

1 whole chicken, washed and cut into 8 pieces
salt and black pepper, to taste
1 onion, finely diced
olive oil
550 g (20 oz, 2½ cups) medium-grain rice

Preheat the oven to 200°C (400°F/Gas mark 6).

Place the chicken into a large stockpot with 3 litres (5 pints) water (add extra water to make enough stock for the soup as well, if desired). Bring to the boil and simmer until the chicken is tender. Skim the stock while it is cooking. Remove the chicken and put aside.

Sieve the stock and season with salt and pepper to taste.

Sauté the onions in a large baking dish with a little olive oil until soft. Add the rice. Gradually add the stock to the rice, stirring continuously; about 1.25 litres (2 pints) should do. Carefully place the chicken pieces into the pan.

Cook in the oven for approximately 20 minutes, or until the rice is cooked and the stock absorbed.

Serve warm with a lettuce salad or steamed broccoli dressed with salt, olive oil and a squeeze of lemon.

Baccala is something my husband would never tire of. It is important to soak the cod in cold water overnight, changing the water as regularly as possible so you can remove as much of the salt as you can.

Baccala with skordalia

900 g (2 lb) salt cod
plain (all-purpose) flour for coating
olive oil
black pepper, to taste
Skordalia (see Starters)

Cut the cod into pieces and soak in cold water overnight.

Remove from the water and dry with paper towels. Coat in the flour and fry in hot olive oil until golden brown, turning once.

Place on kitchen paper to remove any excess oil.

Season with some black pepper and serve with skordalia.

This dish is perfect as is, served simply with some crusty bread.

Pork and cabbage casserole

olive oil
1 small onion, finely diced
1.3 kg (3 lb) shoulder pork,
cut into pieces
300 ml (½ pint) tomato
passata or a 400 g (14 oz)
can diced tomatoes
1 teaspoon sweet paprika
salt and pepper, to taste
1 cabbage (approximately
1.8 kg, 4 lb), shredded

Heat the olive oil in a large casserole dish and sauté the onion. Add pork and cook until browned through. Add the tomato, paprika (if you like a bit of heat you can add a little hot paprika or chilli at this stage) and season with salt and pepper.

Add the shredded cabbage on top of the pork. Pour over 500 ml (16 fl oz, 2 cups) water and cover. Allow to cook slowly until both meat and cabbage are tender, approximately 1½–2 hours. Check to see if more liquid is needed while cooking.

I love this dish served simply with fresh crusty bread, soaking up all the juices.

I love this rich dish and the sweetness of the cooked onions and the exotic aromas of the spices. This dish is often made with rabbit too. Serve with your favourite bread and a green salad.

Beef stifado
beef and onion stew

1.8 kg (4 lb) pickling onions
olive oil
900 g (2 lb) stewing beef or veal, cut into chunks
680 ml (22 fl oz) tomato passata
60 ml (2 fl oz, ¼ cup) red wine
salt, to taste
3 bay leaves
10 peppercorns
6 whole cloves
½ teaspoon cinammon
2 garlic cloves, finely chopped

Peel and discard the tops and tails of the onions.

In a large casserole dish, heat some olive oil and brown the meat. Add the onions. Pour in the tomato passata and 500 ml (16 fl oz, 2 cups) water and wine. Season with salt, add the bay leaves, cloves, cinammon, garlic and peppercorns.

Cover and simmer for about 1–1½ hours, or until the meat and onions are tender and soft.

Serve hot.

This is so simple. I love the flavours in this colourful mix of vegetables. Perfect as is or served with grilled or roasted meat.

Baked vegetables

2 eggplants (aubergines)
3–4 zucchinis (courgettes)
2 green capsicum (bell peppers)
2 red capsicum (bell peppers)
3 large potatoes
3–4 carrots
2 onions, sliced
3 garlic cloves, diced
olive oil
oregano
salt and pepper, to taste
lemon juice

Preheat the oven to 200°C (400°F/Gas mark 6).

Wash the eggplant, zucchini and capsicum and chop into large chunks. Peel and chop the potatoes and carrots. Peel and slice the onions and garlic.

Place all the vegetables in a large baking dish. Pour over a little olive oil to coat the vegetables. Season with oregano, salt, pepper and a squeeze of lemon juice.

Mix well and bake for about 45 minutes, or until all the vegetables are cooked. If it looks a little dry you can add a little water while baking.

Serve warm or at room temperature.

The sweetness of fresh tomatoes is gorgeous in this dish if you have some on hand, otherwise canned tomatoes also work well.

Green bean casserole

1 onion, finely diced
olive oil
1 x 400 g (14 oz) can chopped tomatoes (or 4–5 fresh tomatoes, roughly chopped)
900 g (2 lb) green (French) bean, washed and halved
4 carrots, peeled and sliced
4 small zucchini (courgettes), cut into chunks
salt and pepper, to taste
oregano

Sauté the onion in a casserole dish with a little olive oil until soft. Add tomatoes, beans, carrots and zucchini, season with salt, pepper and oregano. Add 250 ml (8 fl oz/ 1 cup) water, enough to just cover the vegetables. Cover and simmer for approximately 45 minutes, or until tender.

You can add potatoes into this casserole, if you like, or simply serve with mashed potatoes and roasted meat or lamb chops. This is also delicious with fresh crusty bread and lots of feta cheese.

This delicious, simple spinach and rice combination is perfect for a light lunch, an entrée or as a side to a roast, or grilled lamb cutlets. I love to eat it as is with a squeeze of lemon.

Spanakorizo
spinach and rice

1 small onion, finely diced
olive oil
1 bunch spinach
250 ml (8 fl oz, 1 cup) tomato passata
salt and pepper, to taste
125 g (4 oz, ½ cup) medium-grain rice

Sauté the onion in a large casserole dish with a little olive oil.

Meanwhile, wash the spinach and chop roughly into pieces.

Add the tomato to the onions, together with the spinach. Season with salt and pepper and stir. Add the rice and 500 ml (16 fl oz, 2 cups) water, stir and allow to simmer, covered, until the rice is cooked, about 20 minutes. Add more water if it looks too dry.

Serve while hot, but it can also be served cold.

Serve with feta cheese and olives.

See picture next page.

This tasty bean dish is lovely with a simple lettuce salad as a vegetarian dish, or as a side to grilled meats.

Baked beans

450 g (1 lb) lima or butter beans
1 medium onion, finely diced
3 garlic cloves, finely diced
olive oil
2 celery stalks
1 carrot
salt and pepper, to taste
oregano
1 teaspoon sugar
large handful of parsley, chopped
1 x 400 g (14 oz) can diced tomatoes

Soak the beans overnight.

Preheat the oven to 200°C (400°F/Gas mark 6).

Sauté the onion and garlic in a large baking dish with a little olive oil.

Wash and slice the celery. Peel and slice the carrots. Add the vegetables, together with the beans, to the baking dish. Season with salt, pepper, oregano and sugar. Stir in the parsley. Pour in the diced tomatoes and combine and add 250 ml (8 fl oz, 1 cup) water.

Bake for 1 hour, or until the beans are tender and the liquid is absorbed. Add more water if it looks too dry.

Serve hot.

I remember those mornings when my mother would call to tell me that today she was going to be making pita, and if I had time I could go and help her.

My mother's kitchen was inviting... filled with warmth and comfort. I loved being among the chatter and laughter, my mother in charge and instructing my father and myself on the jobs to be done. She would have bowls of fillings arranged on the kitchen bench. Simple feta cheese... my father's favourite, unsophisticated but delicious. At times she would make the cheese pitas, other times she would vary them: spinach, leeks or caramelised onions.

I loved watching her organisation. Balls of dough lined on a tablecloth rested in one corner of the kitchen, fillings were prepared in another. Among all this activity, dough would be rolled out into paper-thin sheets, ready to assemble the pita.

At the appropriate time we would have a coffee break, usually requested by my father. I remember those days fondly: sipping coffee, chatting and waiting for the first pita to be cooked and taken out of the oven. Waiting for the first bite into a slice of the pita, crispy pastry and mouth-watering fillings, savouring every delicious morsel. Of course, I would take a tray or two home for my family to enjoy.

These are the memories that I love so much.

I remember being in my mother's kitchen and lending a hand when she made her filo pastry. We would mix, knead and roll out pastry. I would take instructions and, at the same time, we would chat about anything and everything.

Homemade filo

450 g (1 lb) strong white plain (all-purpose) flour
2 teaspoons salt
1 teaspoon sugar
2 teaspoons baking powder
2 tablespoons olive oil

Sift the flour into a large mixing bowl with the salt, sugar and baking powder. Make a well in the centre and pour in the olive oil, and 250 ml (8 fl oz, 1 cup) warm water. Mix the flour into the liquid mixture slowly, adding more water if required.

Knead the mixture into a soft, elastic dough. Make a ball with the dough. Leave in the bowl, cover with a cloth and allow to rest for at least an hour.

When ready to use, divide the dough into small balls and roll out into sheets using a long thin rolling pin. Keep rolling in all directions until you have made a large, round, very fine sheet. Brush each sheet with a little melted butter and olive oil.

To make pita filo, which separates during baking, stack three or four balls of dough on each other, brushed with a little melted butter mixed with olive oil. Roll this stack into a sheet.

Spanakopita is perfect as a meze or on its own, served simply with some tzatziki for a light lunch.

Spanakopita

spinach pie

200 g (7 oz) melted butter mixed with 125 ml (4 fl oz, ½ cup) olive oil
450 g (1 lb) spinach
300 g (11 oz) feta cheese (if you prefer, you can use ricotta cheese instead of the feta or a combination of both, which is what I like to do)
3 eggs
pinch of nutmeg
125 ml (4 fl oz, ½ cup) milk
black pepper, to taste
filo pastry

Preheat the oven to 200°C (400°F/Gas mark 6).

Prepare a large baking dish by brushing it with a little melted butter and oil.

Wash the spinach, squeeze out the water, dry and chop roughly. Place into a large bowl. Add crumbled feta cheese, eggs, nutmeg and milk. Mix well. Season with black pepper.

Place a sheet of the pita filo or 6–8 sheets prepared filo pastry into the baking dish. Pour the spinach mixture over, then cover with more filo.

Score the pastry and brush with butter/oil mixture. Moisten the edges and crimp together. Sprinkle with a little water before putting into the oven.

Bake for about 30–40 minutes, or until pastry is golden and crispy.

Remove from the oven and sprinkle with some more water. Serve immediately with tzatziki.

You can also make individual spanakopitas by cutting the filo into strips and placing 1 tablespoon of filling at one end, then folding the right corner over to the left to make a triangle. Fold again upwards to make another triangle. Continue until you have a neat triangle parcel.

Brush with butter and oil mixture and cook until golden and crispy.

Tiropitakia
cheese pie

200 g (7 oz) melted butter mixed with 125 ml (4 fl oz, ½ cup) olive oil
300 g (11 oz) feta or ricotta cheese (whichever you prefer, or a combination of both)
3 eggs
125 ml (4 fl oz, ½ cup) milk
filo pastry

Preheat the oven to 200°C (400°F/Gas mark 6).

Prepare a large baking dish by brushing with a little melted butter and oil.

In a bowl mix the cheese, eggs and milk well.

Place 6–8 sheets filo pastry into the prepared baking dish. Pour the cheese mixture over, then cover with more filo.

Score the pastry and brush with the remaining butter/oil mixture. Moisten the edges together and crimp. Sprinkle with a little water before putting into the oven, this helps to prevent the filo pastry curling up too much.

Bake for about 30–40 minutes, or until the pastry is golden and crispy.

Take out of the oven and sprinkle again with a little water. Serve immediately.

You can make individual tiropitakia (cheese triangles) following the method used to make individual spanakopita.

Prassopita
leek pie

200 g (7 oz) melted butter
mixed with 115 ml (4 fl oz,
½ cup) olive oil
900 g (2 lb) leeks
1 tablespoon butter
400 g (14 oz) feta cheese
4 eggs
250 ml (8 fl oz, 1 cup) milk
salt and pepper, to taste
filo pastry

Preheat the oven to 200°C (400°F/Gas mark 6).

Prepare a large baking dish by brushing with a little melted butter and oil.

Wash, then finely chop the leeks. Tip into a pan with the butter and sauté until softened. Remove from the heat and place in a large mixing bowl. Add the feta, eggs, milk and seasoning.

Place 6–8 sheets filo pastry into the prepared baking dish. Pour the leek mixture over, then cover with more filo.

Score the pastry and brush with the remaining butter/ oil mixture. Moisten the edges and crimp together. Sprinkle with a little water before putting into the oven.

Bake for 30–40 minutes, or until the pastry is golden and crispy. Once you have removed the dish from the oven sprinkle again with a little water. Serve immediately.

Onion pie

200 g (7 oz) melted butter
mixed with 125 ml (4 fl oz,
½ cup) olive oil
900 g (2 lb) onions
1 tablespoon butter
400 g (14 oz) feta cheese
4 eggs
250 ml (8 fl oz, 1 cup) milk
salt and pepper, to taste
filo pastry

Preheat the oven to 200°C (400°F/Gas mark 6).

Prepare a large baking dish by brushing with a little melted butter and oil.

Wash and finely chop the onions. Tip into a pan with the butter and sauté until softened. Remove from the heat and place in a large mixing bowl. Add the feta, eggs, milk and seasoning.

Place 6–8 sheets filo pastry into the prepared baking dish. Pour the onion mixture over, then cover with more filo.

Score the pastry and brush with remaining butter/oil mixture. Moisten the edges and crimp togethr. Sprinkle with a little water.

Bake for 30–40 minutes, or until the pastry is golden and crispy. Sprinkle with a little water again once you have taken the pie out of the oven. Serve immediately.

I recall being in my mother's kitchen when the children were small. She would be cooking chips for them. They could never wait until she had finished frying all the potatoes, instead they would eat while she cooked.

Fried potatoes

6–8 large potatoes
oil, for frying
salt

Wash and peel potatoes and cut into chips.

Pat dry with some kitchen paper. Pour enough oil into a large frying pan to cover the base of the pan generously. When hot, fry the potatoes in small batches, turning carefully and cooking until they are golden and crispy. Remove carefully onto a plate and season with salt.

I loved the way my mother would make this for my children for lunch or just an afternoon snack; a special treat from Yia-Yia.

Fried potatoes with egg

Fried potatoes	When you have fried all the potatoes, remove the excess oil
2–3 eggs	and return them to the frying pan. Beat the eggs and pour
salt	over the potatoes. Stir carefully so the egg coats as many
	potatoes as possible without disturbing them too much.
	Cook until the egg has set. Sprinkle with salt and serve hot.

This is delicious as a starter or as a light lunch with a Greek salad and some fresh crusty bread. I always ask my fishmonger to prepare the squid into rings: one less job for me to do.

Fried calamari

300 ml (11 fl oz) oil
60 g (2 oz) plain (all-purpose) flour
60 g (2 oz) semolina
salt and pepper, to taste
675 g (1½ lb) calamari rings
2 lemons, quartered
1 teaspoon oregano

Heat the oil in a medium frying pan. While the oil is warming, place the flour and semolina into a plastic bag and season with salt and pepper. Add the calamari rings to the bag and toss to coat them evenly.

The oil is ready when it starts to sizzle. Carefully fry the calamari rings, in small batches, for approximately 2–3 minutes, until golden brown and crispy, turning once with a fork. Remove the cooked calamari carefully and place onto a platter surrounded by lemon wedges. Sprinkle with oregano and serve.

I love the kind of cooking where everything is cooked in the one pot. This is a traditional and popular meal and every Greek household has its own version of it. I love it cooked simply and with no fuss, just as my mother did.

Youvesti
lamb with tomatoes and pasta

1 onion, finely chopped
75 ml (2½ fl oz/⅓ cup) olive oil
675 g (1½ lb) shoulder of lamb, trimmed and cut into bite-sized pieces
2 garlic cloves, chopped
1 x 400 g (14 oz) can tomatoes
salt and pepper, to taste
400 g (14 oz) risoni or orzo pasta
feta cheese, to serve

Preheat the oven to 180°C (350°F/Gas mark 4).

Sauté the onion in a large heavy casserole dish with olive oil until soft. Add the meat and cook until browned all over. Add the garlic and cook a little, then add the tomatoes and stir well. Season with salt and pepper.

When all is combined add about 1 litre (1¾ pints, 4 cups) water, cover and bake for approximately 1 hour, or until the meat is tender. When the meat is cooked stir in the pasta and return to the oven for another 20 minutes, or until the pasta is cooked through. Add more water, if required.

Serve with feta cheese crumbled on top. This is delicious with a green salad.

This mouth-watering grilled calamari, served with a Greek salad, is ideal on a hot summer's night: uncomplicated and delicious.

Grilled calamari

675 g (1½ lb) calamari rings
Oil and Lemon Dressing (see
Dressings and Sauces)
oregano

Cook the calamari rings over a hot grill (broiler) or barbeque quickly, turning as soon as you see the edges charring: a couple of minutes will do.

Place onto a platter and pour over the dressing and oregano. Serve immediately.

Great as a meze or, together with a salad and some fresh crusty bread, this makes a delicious light lunch.

This is a simple and delicious family meal and one that my family is happy to eat weekly. I especially love how everything is cooked together on one baking tray.

Roast chicken with potatoes

900 g (2 lb) potatoes
1.3 kg (3 lb) chicken
1 lemon
salt and freshly ground black
pepper, to taste
3 garlic cloves, halved
1 tablespoon oregano
50 ml (1¾ fl oz) olive oil

Preheat the oven to 190°C (375°F/Gas mark 5).

Peel the potatoes and cut into wedges.

Place the chicken in a roasting pan and place the potatoes around it. Squeeze the lemon over the chicken and potatoes and season with salt, pepper, garlic and oregano. Drizzle olive oil over and add 250 ml (8 fl oz/ 1 cup) water to the pan. Cook for about 1½ hours, turning the chicken once and adding a little more water, if needed.

The chicken and potatoes should be a glorious golden colour. Serve with a green salad.

This is my father's version of yiouvetsi. He loved to cook it with keftethes and serve it on the table straight from the oven in its cooking dish, so everyone could help themselves.

Keftethes with risoni

Keftethes (see Starters)
1 large onion, chopped
3 tablespoons olive oil
1 x 400 g (14 oz) can chopped tomatoes
400 g (13 oz) risoni
salt and freshly ground black pepper, to taste

Preheat the oven to 180°C (350°F/Gas mark 4).

Prepare the keftethes mixture and shape into small, oval, egg-like balls. Set aside.

Sauté the onion in a large heavy baking dish in olive oil. When soft, add the tomatoes and combine well. Pour in the risoni and about 1 litre (1¾ pints, 4 cups) hot water and stir. Place the prepared raw keftethes carefully in the dish and place in the oven for about 45 minutes, or until the risoni and keftethes are cooked. Add more water, if required.

Spending time with family in Greece was so very special and dear to me. When I entered my auntie's house for the first time, she greeted me with a kiss and a warm hug, and walked me into her kitchen where we made a coffee and began to get to know each other. She told me that I would be a different person after this trip and she was right. I felt at home even though this was my first visit to Greece.

It was summer when I was there: long days and balmy nights. Over breakfast the conversation revolved around what we were going to have for lunch. Food is a way of life in Greece.

Linking arms with my cousin, we strolled through the town centre and to the market, occasionally being stopped by a friend or relative who would always wish you a good day, a good summer and the usual question `what are you cooking today?' At times we knew what we were making, other times we would decide once we saw what the market had on offer. We went back home to prepare the midday

meal, which was always followed by a rest.

Refreshing watermelon would be cut up at the right time and frappés were made, signalling it was time to get up.

According to my cousins, Florina has the best souvlakia and loukoumades in all of Greece. We had to agree with them. The souvlakia was mouth-watering and the loukoumades heavenly, soaked in sweet honey and dusted with cinammon... one, or even two, is never enough.

Driving from one village to another one evening we were entertained by the magical fireflies, like fairies flying around the trees.

Each village more beautiful than the next... lakes, waterfalls, mountains... enchanting.

These are the memories that have stayed with me.

This is lovely with some grilled lamb chops, or on its own as a starter.

Prasoriso

leeks with rice

1 small onion, finely diced
olive oil
250 ml (8 fl oz, 1 cup)
tomato passata
3 leeks, finely chopped
115 g (4 oz, ½ cup) short-
grain rice
salt and pepper, to taste

Sauté the onion in a large casserole dish with olive oil until soft. Add the tomato passata, leeks and rice and season to taste. Add 500 ml (16 fl oz, 2 cups) water and stir well. Simmer on a stovetop, covered, for about 20 minutes, or until the rice is cooked. Add more water if required.

Serve warm with feta cheese, olives and a Greek salad.

Souvlaki is popular as a fast food — these are quick to cook and taste delicious.

Souvlaki

1.3 kg (3 lb) shoulder lamb, cut into bite-sized cubes
375 ml (12 fl oz, 1½ cups) olive oil
2 lemons
5 garlic cloves, diced
2 tablespoons oregano
250 ml (8 fl oz, 1 cup) red wine
salt and pepper, to taste
12 flat breads
Tzatziki, to serve
½ shredded iceberg lettuce, to serve
6 tomatoes, sliced, to serve
tomato sauce (optional)

Put the meat into a bowl and pour in 125 ml (4 fl oz, ½ cup) of olive oil, juice of 1 lemon, diced garlic, oregano and red wine. Mix well and allow to marinate in the refrigerator for at least a few hours, ideally overnight.

When ready to grill (broil) or barbecue the souvlaki, drain the meat, reserving the marinade, and thread onto skewers. Add the remaining olive oil, juice of another lemon and seasonings to the marinade and mix well. Use this to baste the souvlaki while they cook.

Rest the cooked souvlaki on a plate while grilling (broiling) flat breads. Brush the bread with a little marinade and cook them lightly until golden and warm.

Place the meat from the skewers onto the bread, together with some tzatziki, lettuce and tomatoes.

Add tomato sauce, if desired. Roll up and enjoy.

See picture next page.

This charming, simple dish of hilopites and feta cheese takes me back to my childhood. It's perfect for those times when you need something warm but don't have a lot of time to spend in the kitchen.

Hilopites

egg noodles with cheese

450 g (1 lb) hilopites (egg noodles or tagliatelle)
100 g (3½ oz) butter
salt
feta cheese

Cook the hilopites in a generous amount of boiling water until soft and tender.

Drain the hilopites, reserving a little water. Return to the pan and drop in the butter, stirring to coat. Season with salt. This dish should not be dry but a little sloppy.

Serve hot with lots of crumbled feta cheese on top.

This simple pilaf is perfect with anything that uses rice as an accompaniment. I like to make my own chicken stock, sometimes adding a little sweet paprika for heat.

Pilaf

25 g (1 oz) butter
1 onion, finely diced
(optional)
225 g (8 oz) short-grain rice
1 litre (1¾ pints, 4 cups)
chicken stock
salt, to taste

Preheat the oven to 180°C (350°F/Gas mark 4).

Melt the butter in a casserole dish and sauté the onion. Pour in the rice and stir, combining the rice and butter well. Pour in the stock and season.

Cover the casserole dish with a lid and bake for approximately 40 minutes, or until the rice is cooked and the stock has been absorbed.

Rest for 10 minutes. Fluff the rice with a fork before serving.

This hearty veal stew is lovely with some potatoes and a Greek salad.

Moschari kokkinisto

veal stew

1 large onion, finely chopped
3 tablespoons olive oil
900 g (2 lb) veal, cut into chunks
680 ml (22 fl oz) tomato passata
3 tablespoons parsley, chopped
1 tablespoon oregano
salt and pepper, to taste
splash of red wine

Sauté the onion in a large casserole dish with olive oil until soft. Add meat and fry until browned. Add the tomato passatta, parsley, oregano and season with salt and pepper. Add 250 ml (8 fl oz, 1 cup) water and a splash of red wine.

Cover the casserole dish and simmer on the stove for 1–1½ hours, or until the meat is tender and the sauce has thickened. Add more water while cooking if it gets too dry.

The kitchen table was set beautifully with a perfectly ironed tablecloth, the one with the embroidered flowers around the edge, my mother's favourite. A loaf of Vienna bread, a small bowl of black Kalamata olives and a block of feta cheese; these modest foods were the basis of almost every family meal. There were plates of keftethes, roasted red peppers and salad greens picked from the vegetable garden.

I love the simplicity of meals coming together like this.

Having vegetables so close by, being involved in the planting and reaping the rewards of delicious fresh ingredients is very gratifying.

In the summer months my mother grew tomatoes, cucumbers, lettuce, which she would pick daily for lunch. There were green beans, zucchini and peppers made into delicious meals when they were ready for the picking. Winter would bring caulifowers, cabbages, broccoli and silverbeet to our table.

I remember the enveloping scent of the oregano my mother dried in bunches to be used all year long; the parsley or dill that she would ask me to go and pick for her when needed. When there were generous amounts of figs, tomatoes or peppers, preserves were made.

In the summer months, when the fruit trees were plentiful with plums, quince and apricots, jams and pots of compote were made, which we loved so much served with Greek yogurt and a drizzle of honey.

Our meals reflected what was growing that given month. There is nothing more delightful than a tomato picked straight from the plant, bursting with the flavour of summer and eaten with just a sprinkling of salt. This, for me, is the essence of the Greek kitchen.

Salads

The table is being set for lunch with a welcoming tablecloth, plates, glasses, cutlery and, of course, the big bowl of beautifully dressed salad.

The salad takes its place in the centre of the table where everyone can share. It is always eaten with the main meal and made fresh just before serving. There is nothing more delicious than mopping up the mouth-watering dressing of olive oil and vinegar or lemon with a piece of bread.

The traditional Greek salad is, of course the most well-known and is certainly enjoyed often. Fresh, wholesome and nutritious.

I love the simplicity of this salad. This is the way my mother usually made her salad: in a large bowl, placed in the middle of the table, ready for everyone to share.

Lettuce salad

1 iceberg lettuce
2 tablespoons dill, finely
chopped
extra virgin olive oil
2 tablespoons white wine
vinegar
salt, to taste

Wash and pat dry the lettuce, then shred it finely and place in a bowl with the dill.

Combine the oil, vinegar and salt in a jar and shake. Pour over the lettuce and dill and serve.

When preparing this dish I love to use the leaves as well. I think it is because my mother didn't throw much out. I love the sweetness of the cooked beetroot in this simple salad, together with the sharpness of the vinegar and garlic.

Beetroot salad

900 g (2 lb) beetroot
salt and pepper
100 ml (3½ fl oz) extra virgin olive oil
2 tablespons red wine vinegar
1–2 garlic cloves, chopped (optional)

Wash the beetroot, leaving the skins on. Cut off the tops and tails. Place into a large saucepan with plenty of water and cook until tender.

If using the leaves, wash them and add to the beetroot when almost done.

When the beetroot is tender, drain and peel. Cut into pieces, chop up the leaves and season to taste, adding oil, vinegar and garlic.

This combination may seem a little strange; however, when you want something light, refreshing and with a little tang this is just the thing. Served with crusty bread, it becomes the perfect light lunch or afternoon snack.

Watermelon and feta salad with pomegranate and mint

1 small/medium watermelon
200 g (7 oz) feta, broken into chunks
100 ml (3½ fl oz) extra virgin olive oil
juice of 1 lemon
salt and pepper, to taste
seeds from 1 pomegranate
small bunch of mint, chopped

Cut the watermelon into large chunks and place in a large salad bowl. Add feta cheese and dress with olive oil, lemon juice, salt, pepper, pomegranate seeds and chopped mint.

If you prefer, you can roast the feta in the oven sprinkled with 1 tablespoon of brown sugar (see Starters).

The plump sweetness of both the tomatoes and the eggplant in this salad is what makes it so perfectly summery.

Village-style eggplant salad

2 medium eggplants
(aubergines)
olive oil
salt and freshly ground black
pepper, to taste
salad greens (rocket/arugula
and cos)
4 tomatoes, cut into wedges
1 red onion, sliced
Olive Oil and Vinegar
Dressing (see Dressings and
Sauces)
1 roasted red capsicum (bell
pepper), cut into strips
100 g (3½ oz) feta cheese

Trim the eggplants and cut into cubes. Heat a little olive oil in a large frying pan and fry the cubed eggplant in batches. Drain on kitchen paper. Allow the eggplant to cool and season with a little salt and pepper.

Place the salad greens, tomatoes and onions in a large salad bowl and toss with the dressing.

Add the cooked eggplant, red capsicum and crumble the feta cheese on top. Serve with crusty fresh bread.

Perfect for a simple summer lunch.

Zucchini, are at their best, sweet and delicate, when picked small. This simple salad is delicious served with fish; however, you can serve it with any meat you prefer, or on its own for a healthy vegetarian meal.

Zucchini
salad

900 g (2 lb) small zucchinis
(courgettes)
6 garlic cloves
100 ml (3½ fl oz) extra
virgin olive oil
juice of 1 lemon
salt and freshly ground black
pepper, to taste
½ cup parsley, finely chopped

Wash and cut the zucchini in half. Place into a baking dish, together with the garlic. Add 100 ml (3½ fl oz) water and drizzle with half the olive oil. Bake for 20–30 minutes, turning once, or until tender. Remove from the baking dish and arrange on a platter. Allow to cool.

Whisk the remaining olive oil and lemon juice and pour over. Season to taste and garnish with parsley.

Serve with fish, roast meats or on its own.

Green bean salad

900 g (2 lb) green beans
2 garlic cloves
Oil and Vinegar Dressing
(see Dressings and Sauces)

Wash and trim the green beans, cook in a large pan of boiling water for about 10–15 minutes, keeping them a little firm. Drain carefully and dip in a bowl of cold water. Drain and dry with kitchen paper.

Add garlic to the dressing, combining well.

Place the beans in a bowl, pour the dressing over and serve.

When I was in Greece, I often went for a 'volta', a walk, in the evening with my cousin, arm in arm along the seafront promenade in Thessaloniki. The azure blue sea and the city's landmark, The White Tower, together with the endless amount of cafés and bars in the central city square make Thessaloniki stunning and lively. Rich in culture, this cosmopolitan city is also known for its writers and artists.

I loved getting lost among the specialty food stores full of herbs and spices, and the charming bookstores.

This is a typical Greek salad and I often make it this way, but I do prefer it without the lettuce.

Traditional Greek salad

1 small lettuce (optional)
2 large tomatoes
1 cucumber
1 medium onion
black olives
100 g (3½ oz) feta cheese
Oil and Vinegar Dressing
(see Dressings and Sauces)

Wash and pat dry the lettuce, then cut into pieces. Wash and dry the tomatoes and cut into wedges. Peel the cucumber and onion and slice both finely. Place these into a large salad bowl, adding olives and crumbled feta cheese.

Prepare the oil and vinegar dressing and pour over the salad. Mix well and serve.

Whenever my mother made a cauliflower or broccoli salad she would cook the vegetables until they were very soft—she preferred them that way. Because she loved to grow her own vegetables and eat freshly picked produce, we would have whatever was growing at that time.

Cauliflower salad

1 small cauliflower
Oil and Lemon Dressing (see
Dressings and Sauces)

Wash the cauliflower well and cut into florets. I just snap them apart with my hands. Place into a large pan of boiling water and simmer until tender. When cooked, drain and place into a large salad bowl and drizzle with the oil and lemon dressing.

You may prefer to steam the cauliflower.

This was one of the salads that my mother would make on almost a daily basis in the summer, using the sweet tomatoes she had grown in her own garden.

Domatosalata
tomato and onion salad

6 tomatoes
1 large red onion
Oil and Vinegar Dressing
(see Dressings and Sauces)
oregano (optional)

Chop the tomatoes into wedges. Peel and slice the onion. Toss with oil and vinegar dressing and sprinkle with a little oregano, if desired.

Perfect with grilled (broiled) fish or meats.

Strolling through the cobblestone streets of Fira, Santorini, we found a quaint little family-owned restaurant overlooking the Aegean Sea. Family photos were displayed on the walls and jars of homemade sweets lined the shelves. We ordered a selection of meze plates and this is the salad I loved.

Rocket and orange salad

2 teaspoons Greek honey
1 teaspoon mustard
2 tablespoons vinegar
100 ml (3½ fl oz, ⅔ cup) extra virgin olive oil
2 teaspoons orange juice
2 teaspoons sesame seeds
750 g (1½ lb, 3 cups) rocket (arugula) leaves
500 g (1 lb, 2 cups) salad leaves
2 oranges
250 g (9 oz) Greek Graveria or Kasseri cheese

To make the dressing, whisk the honey, mustard, vinegar, olive oil, orange juice and sesame seeds in a bowl until combined.

Wash the rocket and salad leaves and place onto a large salad platter. Remove the peel from the oranges and slice thinly into rounds, carefully removing any bitter pith. Slice the cheese thinly into bite-sized pieces. Arrange the cheese and orange slices onto the greens and pour over the dressing.

Delicious served with keftethes and fresh crusty bread or as part of a meze meal.

Broccoli salad

900 g (2 lb) broccoli
Oil and Lemon Dressing (see
Dressings and Sauces)

Wash the broccoli well in lots of cold water and break into bite-sized pieces. Place in a large pan of boiling water and cook until tender.

When soft, carefully drain and place into a salad bowl and pour over the dressing.

This is delicious with fish.

There was always horta growing in our vegetable garden and my mother would pick as much as she needed for for her lunch that day, and at other times enough to refrigerate and keep for a couple of days.

Horta salata

endive salad

900 g (2 lb) endives (use spinach, if you prefer)
Oil and Lemon Dressing (see Dressings and Sauces)

Wash the endives well and trim, removing any thick stalks. Place into a large pan of boiling water and simmer for about 20 minutes, or until tender.

Drain well, place into a large serving bowl and allow to cool. Pour over the dressing.

Serve with fish.

Pickled cabbage was always served as a meze together with some black olives, cheese and bread and a glass of ouzo. Perfect on a hot summer's afternoon.

Lahano toursi
pickled cabbage

1 cabbage
½ stick celery
2 litres (3½ pints) white vinegar
1 cup (225 g, 8 oz) sugar
1 cup (250 ml, 8 fl oz) olive oil
½ cup (115 g, 4 oz) sea salt

Wash and chop cabbage roughly into bite-sized pieces. Slice the celery finely and add to the cabbage. Place the vegetables into a large bowl.

Place the vinegar, and an equal quantity of water, the sugar, olive oil and salt into a large pan. Bring to the boil and simmer for a couple of minutes. Pour this liquid onto the cabbage and celery mixture, cover and allow it to marinate overnight.

The next day, transfer the pickled cabbage together with some of the liquid into jars or, alternatvely, leave it in a large bowl. Keep for a couple of weeks in the refrigerator.

I love the taste and aroma of roasted red capsicum and the sweetness of tomatoes. I think they are perfect together.

Roasted red capsicum and tomato salad

6 roasted red capsicums (bell peppers)
6 tomatoes
olive oil
red wine vinegar
2 cloves garlic (optional)
salt
8 basil leaves

Peel and slice the roasted capsicum and allow to cool. Slice the tomatoes into wedges and add to the capsicum. Drizzle over the olive oil and red wine vinegar, to taste. Add garlic, if desired, and season with salt. Tear the basil leaves and combine with the tomatoes and capsicum.

Desserts

I do have a sweet tooth and cannot resist a piece of galahtoboureko. Greek cakes are sweet, sometimes syrupy and definitely tempting. They are best served with a glass of cold water.

At Christmas time most households have baked cookies, such as kourabiedes or melomakarona or both, so that they can be offered to guests during the holiday season with their coffee. And of course, it is always nice to make a few extra batches so they can be enjoyed for weeks after the celebrations are over.

Most Greek pantries are stocked with jars of preserves, which are served to guests with a small spoon on a plate together with a Greek coffee and water.

There is something very comforting in knowing that you have a sweet on hand for that unexpected guest.

I love how simple this cake is to make. It is very typically Greek and a charming family treat. Every Greek household has its own version of this very sweet cake.

Revani

semolina cake with syrup

500 m (16 fl oz, 2 cups) oil
225 g (8 oz, 1 cup) caster (superfine) sugar
6 eggs
juice of 1 orange
1 teaspoon vanilla extract
225 g (8 oz, 1 cup) semolina
450 g (1 lb, 2 cups) self-raising (self-rising) flour
225 g (8 oz, 1 cup) sugar
lemon zest

Preheat the oven to 200°C (400°F/Gas mark 6).

Using an electric mixer, in a bowl, combine the oil and sugar. Slowly add the eggs, one at a time. Add the orange juice, vanilla, semolina and flour and keep mixing until well combined.

Pour into a prepared baking dish and bake for about 30–40 minutes, or until cooked. Allow to cool.

To prepare the syrup, bring 500 ml (16 fl oz, 2 cups) water, sugar and lemon zest to the boil and simmer for 10 minutes. Pour onto the cake slowly. Once the syrup has been absorbed you can cut the cake into pieces.

Serve at room temperature or cold.

I remember those afternoons when my father would announce that he was making loukoumades—his specialty—and we would wait with anticipation for these moreish treats. They are so exotically sweet and delicious with a cup of Greek coffee.

Loukoumades
honey doughnuts

2 tablespoons dry yeast
350 g (12 oz, 3 cups) plain (all-purpose) flour
1 tablespoon sugar
1 teaspoon salt
250 ml (8 fl oz, 1 cup) warm milk
olive oil
honey (warmed)
cinnamon

Sift all the dry ingredients into a large mixing bowl, add 1 cup (250 ml, 8 fl oz) warm milk and mix into a smooth batter.

Cover and let rest until it has doubled in size, approximately 1½ hours. Make sure the dough is in a warm place.

In a large pan, pour enough oil for frying. Take small handfuls of dough and slowly drop them into the hot oil. Cook until golden brown.

Place onto a serving dish. Drizzle with warm honey and sprinkle with plenty of ground cinnamon.

Serve immediately.

This sweet creamy rizogalo fills me with childhood memories. It is delicious eaten warm or cold out of the refrigerator the next day.

Rizogalo

rice pudding

140 g (5 oz) medium-grain rice
600 ml (20 fl oz) full-fat (whole) milk
30 gm (1 oz) cornflour (cornstarch)
140 gm (5 oz) caster (superfine) sugar
ground cinnamon, to serve

Put the rice and 300 ml (10 fl oz) water into a saucepan and simmer over a low heat until the rice is cooked and the water has been absorbed.

Add the milk slowly and keep stirring.

Mix the cornflour with a little water to make a paste and add to the rice mixture, together with the sugar. Keep stirring until it thickens.

When ready, pour into individual bowls and serve with plenty of ground cinnamon.

I love these biscuits. They are perfect with a cup of tea or coffee and they really do melt in the mouth. My mother always had a plate of these on hand, ready for that unexpected visitor.

Kourabiedes
biscuits in icing sugar

225 g (8 oz) unsalted butter
115 g (4 oz, ½ cup) caster
(superfine) sugar
3 egg yolks
125 ml (4 fl oz, ½ cup) oil
30 ml (1 fl oz) ouzo
1 small teaspoon baking
powder
450–550 g(16–20 oz, 4–5
cups) plain (all-purpose) flour
75 gm (2½ oz) slivered
almonds (optional)
icing (confectioners') sugar,
for dusting

Preheat the oven to 200°C (400°F/Gas mark 6).

In a bowl, cream the butter and sugar until light and fluffy. Add the egg yolks and mix well. Pour in the oil, ouzo and baking powder.

Slowly fold in the flour a little at a time. You may not need all the flour; the dough needs to be light and not sticky. Do not overwork the dough as this can make the kourabiedes tough.

Take a small handful of dough and shape into crescents. Place them onto a baking tray.

Place the slivered almonds in a clean frying pan and toast them over a low heat on the stove top until slighty golden. Sprinkle over the dough.

Bake for about 20 minutes, or until golden brown. Remove from the oven and, using a spatula, transfer onto baking paper. When they are cool, dust with plenty of icing sugar and transfer onto a platter.

These cookies keep well for about 3–4 weeks.

This gorgeous cake is perfect for any special occasion. The blend of cinnamon, walnuts and honey make this cake irresistible. It is very typical of Greek cakes.

Karydopita
walnut cake with syrup

75 g (2½ oz) unsalted butter
150 gm (5 oz) caster (superfine) sugar
3 eggs, separated
75 g (2½ oz) self-raising (self-rising) flour
75 g (2½ oz) semolina
1 teaspoon cinnamon
140 g (5 oz) walnuts, finely chopped
125 ml (4 fl oz, ½ cup) full-fat (whole) milk
225 g (8 oz, 1 cup) caster (superfine) sugar
lemon zest
4 cloves

Preheat the oven to 200°C (400°F/Gas mark 6).

Cream the butter and sugar in a large mixing bowl. Add the egg yolks and beat until well combined. Add the flour, semolina and cinnamon and mix well. Add the walnuts and milk. Whisk the egg whites until light and fluffy and fold into the mixture.

Pour into a lightly buttered baking dish and bake for about 45 minutes, or until cooked.

Pour 500 ml (16 fl oz, 2 cups) water, sugar, lemon zest and cloves into a small saucepan. Simmer over gentle heat for about 10 minutes. Pour over the cake carefully. Leave for about an hour, then cut into pieces. Serve at room temperature or cold.

I love the way my mother made her halva and this is the way I make it for my family. It is a very typical Greek dessert and most Greek homes would have their own variation.

Halva

560 g (20 oz, 2½ cups) caster (superfine) sugar
1 cinnamon stick
lemon peel (¼ lemon)
6–8 whole cloves
250 ml (8 fl oz, 1 cup) vegetable oil
500 g (16 oz, 2 cups) semolina
115 g (4 oz, ½ cup) chopped almonds (optional)
ground cinnamon, to serve

Put 1 litre (1¾ pints, 4 cups) water and sugar in a large saucepan and stir until the sugar is dissolved. Add the cinnamon stick, lemon peel and cloves, cover and boil for about 5–7 minutes.

In a large pan, heat the oil, add the semolina and brown a little, stirring continuously. Add the almonds, if desired

Remove the spices from the syrup and slowly start adding the liquid to the semolina mixture. Stir until all the syrup is absorbed and the semolina is puffed and soft. It should fall off the spoon cleanly.

Remove from the heat and allow to stand for about 10 minutes, then transfer into a large mould or small, individual moulds. Leave to rest on the work surface. When the halva feels firm and has set, unmould and sprinkle with ground cinnamon to decorate.

Serve warm or cold.

This is my favourite Greek dessert and I love making it. It is just the thing that appeals to my sweet tooth.

Galahtohoureko

custard pie with syrup

5 eggs

225 g (8 oz, 1 cup) caster (superfine) sugar

500 g (16 oz, 2 cups) semolina

1 teaspoon vanilla extract

3 litres (5 pints) full-fat (whole) milk (warm)

200 g (7 oz) filo pastry

75 ml (2½ fl oz, ⅓ cup) butter, melted

350 g (12 oz, 1½ cups) caster (superfine) sugar

lemon zest

Preheat the oven to 200°C (400°F/Gas mark 6).

In a bowl, beat the eggs and sugar until light and creamy. Add the semolina and vanilla and mix well. Pour the mixture into a large saucepan and slowly pour in the warm milk, stirring continuously over a low heat. Keep mixing until the mixture is a smooth thick custard. Remove from the heat.

In a large baking dish, place half the filo sheets, brushing with the melted butter as you go. Pour in the custard and spread evenly. Continue with the remaining filo sheets. Brush the top layer with melted butter and sprinkle with a little water.

Bake for about 30 minutes, or until golden brown. Remove from oven and allow to cool.

To prepare the syrup, bring 500 ml (16 fl oz, 2 cups) water, the sugar and a little lemon zest to the boil and simmer for 10 minutes. Pour over the cake. When all the syrup has been absorbed and the cake is cool, cut into pieces. Serve warm or cold.

I love the simplicity of this cake. I always add the sultanas (golden raisins). Perfect with a cup of tea or coffee.

Olive oil cake

250 ml (8 fl oz, 1 cup) olive oil
225 g (8 oz, 1 cup) sugar
3 eggs
250 ml (8 fl oz, 1 cup) milk
self-raising (self-rising) flour
115 g (4 oz, ½ cup) sultanas (golden raisins) (optional)
zest of ½ lemon

Preheat the oven to 200°C (400°F/Gas mark 6). Lightly grease and line a 23 cm (9 in) round cake tin.

Using an electric mixer, combine the oil and sugar in a bowl. Add the eggs in, one at a time, and then the milk. Add as much flour as necessary to make a smooth cake mixture. Add the sultanas and zest of half a lemon and mix well.

Pour the mixture into a prepared cake tin and bake for 45–60 minutes or until cooked.

Serve warm or cold.

I like to serve these pancakes simply with a sprinkling of sugar. If you prefer, you can drizzle honey and some cinammon on them, which is also lovely.

Pancakes

3 eggs
250 ml (8 fl oz, 1 cup) milk
225 g (8 oz, 2 cups) self-raising (self-rising) flour
3 tablespoons oil
sugar, to serve
cinammon, to serve

Beat the eggs and add a little milk followed by some flour. Keep adding milk and flour alternately until you have a thick and smooth batter.

In a large frying pan, heat the oil and pour in heaped spoonfuls of the batter. Do not crowd the pan as the pancakes will spread. Cook on both sides, until they are golden, turning only once.

Place on a serving plate and sprinkle simply with sugar or, if you prefer, ground cinammon.

My parents had a beautiful plum tree in their backyard and when there was extra fruit my mother would make a delicious compote. I love this plum compote served simply with some Greek yogurt.

Plum compote

450 g(1 lb, 2 cups) caster
(superfine) sugar
lemon zest
12 red plums
cinammon stick

Wash the plums and halve them, removing the pits.

Pour 1 litre (1¾ pints, 4 cups) water, the sugar, a couple of strips of lemon zest and a cinammon stick into a large pan.

Bring to the boil, then add the plums and simmer until they are just tender but not falling apart, about 7–10 minutes. Remove the fruit and decant into a glass jar using a slotted spoon. Allow the syrup to cool, then pour over the fruit.

Serve at room temperature.

This is also delicious served cold from the refrigerator on a warm day, topped with yogurt.

This keeps well for 4–5 days in the refrigerator.

These golden honey biscuits are sweet and fragrant. My mother had a special small glass dish that had a star shaped pattern on the bottom. I would press this dish onto the biscuits to decorate them.

Melomakarona

honey cookies

900 g (2 lb, 4 cups) plain (all-purpose) flour
1 teaspoon baking powder
250 ml (8 fl oz, 1 cup) oil
115 g (4 oz, ½ cup) caster (superfine) sugar
125 ml (4 fl oz, ½ cup) orange juice
1 teaspoon orange zest, grated
250 ml (8 fl oz, 1 cup) honey
225 g (8 oz, 1 cup) caster (superfine) sugar
115 g (4 oz, ½ cup) walnuts, finely chopped and mixed with 1 teaspoon cinnamon

Preheat the oven to 200°C (400°F/Gas mark6).

Sift the flour and baking powder into a large mixing bowl. Make a well in the centre and add the oil, sugar, orange juice and zest. Using your hands, combine and knead lightly until the dough is smooth and greasy. You can either use a cookie cutter or simply roll out small balls of the dough in your hands and and flatten them a little. Traditionally they should be an oval shape. Dot with a fork to make a pattern of spots on top.

Line baking sheets with baking paper and place dough on the tray. Bake for about 30 minutes, or until golden.

Pour the honey, sugar and 250 ml (8 fl oz, 1 cup) water in a large pan and simmer for about 8 minutes. Pour the syrup over the cookies as soon as they come out of the oven. When the syrup has been absorbed, turn the cookies over and allow to cool. Turn right side up and decorate with the walnut and cinnamon mixture. Place on a serving dish.

This sweet preserve is something that most Greek households would have in the refrigerator. It is typically served with a small spoon on a small glass dish, with a cup of Greek coffee and a glass of cold water.

Orange rind preserve in syrup

900 g (2 lb) oranges (thick skinned)
900 g (2 lb) caster (superfine) sugar
2 tablespoons lemon juice

Wash the oranges and scrub them with a fine grater. Using a sharp knife, score the zest into 8 and remove carefully. Roll these into tight scrolls and thread them onto a large piece of cotton using a large needle, making a necklace of orange zest rolls.

In a large saucepan, add enough water to cover the orange peel. Bring to the boil and simmer for about 4 minutes, Drain in a colander and repeat the process to remove any bitterness.

In another pan, pour in 625 ml (20 fl oz, 2½ cups) water and sugar. Simmer for about 10 minutes to make a syrup.

Take the orange peel rolls carefully off the cotton and place into the syrup. Simmer for 15 minutes, or until the syrup has thickened. Add the lemon juice and put into sterilised jars while still hot. Allow to rest overnight, then store in the refrigerator.

Quince preserve in syrup

1 kg (2 lb) quince
3 tablespoons lemon juice
1 kg (2 lb) caster sugar

Peel and grate or chop quince roughly and place into a saucepan with 3 cups (750 ml, 24 fl oz) water and lemon juice. Simmer until the quince is soft and the water has almost been absorbed.

I love the rich colour the quince turns once cooked.

Pour in sugar, combine careully and allow to stand overnight.

In the morning, place back onto a low heat and simmer until the quince is cooked and translucent and the syrup has thickened. Pour into sterilised jars and allow to cool. Store in the refrigerator.

This simple and tasty compote is delicious served with Greek yogurt ... just the way my family likes to eat it, for breakfast or dessert or simply as a snack at any time of the day.

Pears and raspberries compote

5–6 medium pears
225 g (8 oz) fresh raspberries
sugar, to taste
squeeze of lemon
cinammon stick (optional)

Peel and core the pears and cut them into slices or chunks. Place in a pan together with raspberries, sugar, a squeeze of lemon juice, the cinammon stick and enough water to cover.

Cook over medium heat until the pears are tender but not mushy, about 15 minutes. Add a little more water, if needed. Add sugar to taste.

When ready, remove from heat and allow to cool before serving.

Perfect with Greek yogurt.

I love the taste of this homemade yogurt. You cannot compare it to commercially ones; there is something homely about it. I love to sit down for lunch with a bowl of yogurt and a slice of tiropita. Nothing could be more delicious.

Yogurt

2 litres (1¾ pints) full-fat (whole) milk
75 ml (2½ fl oz, ⅓ cup) natural (plain) yogurt

Boil the milk and allow to cool to a lukewarm temperature. Stir the yogurt into a little lukewarm milk. This is used to make a culture. Add the remaining milk slowly and stir well.

Pour into cups, jars or individual bowls. Cover with baking paper and, using either a tablecloth or kitchen towels, cover and keep warm for at least 4 hours. I like to place a folded tablecloth on my kitchen bench, place my jars on it and cover with another tablecloth, so they keep warm all around.

By this time the yogurt should begin to set. Place the jars into the refrigerator. The yogurt should keep for about 1 week. Keep a little of your homemade yogurt to use as a culture for your next batch.

I especially love my yogurt drizzled with honey and sprinkled with cinammon.

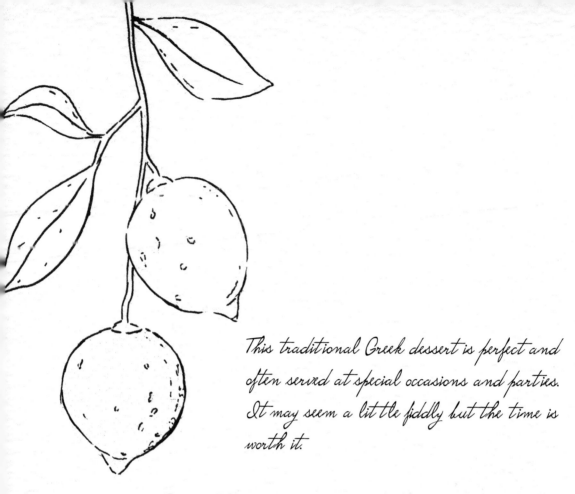

This traditional Greek dessert is perfect and often served at special occasions and parties. It may seem a little fiddly but the time is worth it.

Baklava

900 g (2 lb, 4 cups) walnuts, chopped
1 tablespoon cinnamon
225 g (8 oz) clarified unsalted butter (melt the butter and spoon out any creamy solids)
1–2 packets filo pastry
whole cloves, to decorate
675 g (1½ lb, 3 cups) sugar
125 ml (4 fl oz, ½ cup) honey
lemon zest

Preheat the oven to 180°C (350°F/Gas mark 4).

Combine the nuts and cinammon in a large bowl. Using the melted butter, grease a baking tray and arrange a sheet of filo pastry in it. Brush the filo with the butter and repeat until you have arranged 6 sheets.

Scatter some of the nut mixture and then arrange another 2 sheets on top, brushing each with the butter. Continue layering the nut mixture and filo pastry until you have used up all the nuts. Finish off with another 6 sheets, again brushing with the melted butter after each filo sheet.

Using a sharp knife, score the top layers into diamond shapes and sprinkle with some cold water so the filo doesn't curl while baking. Decorate each diamond with a clove.

Bake for 30 minutes, then turn the oven temperature down to 140°C (275°F/Gas mark 1) and bake for another 30 minutes, or until golden brown. Allow to cool while preparing the syrup.

Place the sugar, honey, lemon zest and 500 ml (16 fl oz, 2 cups) water into a saucepan and simmer for about 5–7 minutes. Carefully ladle the hot syrup onto the baklava, allowing it to absorb the syrup evenly. Let cool before serving.

See picture next page.

In a Greek household, drinking coffee is a way of life. Men would sit and discuss politics over a cup of coffee and ouzo. The women would exchange recipes or simply chat about their day.

Greek coffee

2 teaspoons sugar
2 teaspoons Greek coffee

Greek coffee is brewed in a long-handled copper (or stainless steel) classic 'briki' (coffee pot).

Pour 500 ml (16 fl oz, 2 cups) water into the briki. Add sugar and coffee and stir well. Place over a low heat and allow to simmer. Before it starts to boil, remove from the heat and pour the froth into 2 coffee cups. Return to the stove and allow to boil, then carefully pour the coffee into the cups. Take care not to disturb the froth too much.

Easter
Festival Food

Memories of Easter have been fused into my mind.

Easter is the most significant religious celebration in the Greek Orthodox faith. The Lenten fast begins seven weeks before Easter on a Monday known as 'Clean Monday'. This is a time to cleanse the body and spirit. During this fasting you abstain from foods that contain red blood, meat, poultry, milk, cheese and eggs.

Easter preparations begin on Holy Thursday when the eggs are dyed red to represent the blood of Christ. My mother would also decorate a few using a leaf from her garden as a stencil. She would place the leaf on a clean egg, put it into a stocking, tie it tightly and slowly immerse it into the red dye. When the eggs were ready and the leaves removed she would polish them with a little olive oil. They would then take their place in a large bowl.

Women in Greek families are busy at this time of year baking tsourekia and koulouria. The house is filled with aromas of mahlepi and warm tsoureki straight out of the oven. I now spend Holy Thursday dyeing eggs and baking with my daughters. My kitchen becomes a hive of conversation and laughter.

Good Friday is the holiest day of the Easter calendar. It is a day of mourning, when traditional foods, such as lentil soup, are eaten. There is a church service in the afternoon, which families attend to help decorate the Epitaphio (the tomb of Christ) with fresh flowers. Later, they return for the evening service, when the priest and choir chant Byzantine hymns. During this service the Epitaphio is taken out of the church for a procession and all follow, holding their lit candles to symbolise the mourners.

On Holy Saturday the Mayiritsa (Easter soup) is cooked and the house prepared for the coming feast.

Families then attend church for the Resurrection service. Just before midnight, the church is darkened and everyone is silent. The flickering 'Eternal Flame' (a candle inside the altar) is the only light. At midnight the priest lights his candle from the Eternal Flame and sings

'Christos Anesti'. 'Christ is risen'. The priest holds out his candle and the flame is given to the closest person. This flame travels throughout the entire church while everyone chants 'Christos Anesti'. We then take our lit candles home and place them near our icons.

Easter Sunday is a day to be spent with family and friends and every soul feasts on lamb, usually cooked on a spit or, at times, oven-roasted. Everyone always loves the part where the red eggs are cracked. From ancient times, the egg has been a symbol of the renewal of life. The message of the red eggs is victory over death and Christ breaking free from the tomb. As a child I just wanted to have the strongest egg.

This traditional Greek Easter bread is one of the things that my family looks forward to at Easter time. The exotic mahlepi fragrance reminds me of Easter. I love this bread and could eat it all year around.

Tsourekia

Easter bread

225 g (8 oz) fresh yeast
1 teaspoon salt
1 teapoon sugar
flour
900 g (2 lb, 4 cups) caster
(superfine) sugar
450 g (1 lb) unsalted butter,
melted
pinch of salt
1 tablespoon ground mahlepi
(from specialty Greek or
Middle Eastern stores)
vanilla extract
750 ml (24 fl oz, 3 cups)
warm full-fat (whole) milk
375 ml (12 fl oz, 1½ cups)
fresh orange juice
12 eggs
plain (all-purpose) flour
2 egg yolks, beaten with a
little warm water
sesame seeds

Preheat the oven to 200°C (400°F/Gas mark 6).

Prepare the yeast mixture by combining fresh yeast, salt, sugar, 250 ml (8 fl oz, 1 cup) warm water and enough flour to make a paste. Leave in a covered bowl in a warm place until doubled in size, about 30 minutes.

In a large bowl, mix the sugar and melted butter together. Add the salt, mahlepi and vanilla. Pour in the warm milk and fresh orange juice and, using your hand, mix all the ingredients together. Add the eggs, one at a time, again mixing with your hand. Add the yeast mixture. Slowly start adding flour, combining ingredients well as you go. Use as much flour as required to make a warm, soft and sticky dough. Be careful not to overwork the dough.

Place the dough back into the basin and cover well, using baking paper and blankets. Allow to rest for about 2 hours, or until it has tripled in size.

Take the dough from the basin and divide into small balls on a smooth floured working surface. Roll three balls out into long cylinders and braid (plait) them together. Place the bread on a greased and lined baking sheet and leave in a warm place for about 30 minutes, or until doubled in size. I like to coat my hands with a little warm olive oil when rolling and braiding the bread so it doesn't get too sticky.

Brush the tops of the loaves with a little beaten egg yolk and water mixture and sprinkle with sesame seeds. Bake for about 30 minutes, or until cooked. Cool on wire racks.

Koulouria

Easter cookies

140 g (5 oz) unsalted butter
225 g (8 oz, 1 cup) sugar
2 eggs
½ teaspoon vanilla extract
250 ml (8 fl oz, 1 cup) orange juice
250 ml (8 fl oz, 1 cup) oil
self-raising (self-rising) flour
2 egg yolks, beaten

Preheat the oven to 220°C (420°F/Gas mark 7).

Cream the butter and sugar in a large bowl. Add the eggs one at a time and beat well. Add the vanilla, orange juice and oil. Combine well.

Start adding the flour, a little at a time, mixing continuously with one hand. Add as much flour as required to form a smooth dough that is not sticky. Avoid overworking the mixture as that will make the cookies tough.

Take pieces of the dough and, on a smooth surface, roll into a cylinder, fold in half and twist. Continue until all the dough is finished.

Place on a baking sheet lined with baking paper. Brush the tops of the cookies with beaten egg yolks and bake for about 20 minutes, or until golden brown.

Traditionally you would use lamb intestines, tripe, heart, liver and kidneys in this soup. Then the lamb would be cooked on a spit for Easter lunch. I don't use all of the organs, just the liver and kidneys to give it an authentic flavour.

Mayeritsa
Greek Easter soup

250 g (9 oz) lamb livers
250 g (9 oz) lamb kidneys
olive oil
115 g (4 oz, ½ cup) dill, finely chopped
115 g (4 oz, ½ cup) spring onions (scallions), chopped
½ iceberg lettuce, finely chopped
salt and pepper, to taste
115 g (4 oz, ½ cup) medium-grain rice (optional)
Egg and Lemon Sauce (see Dressings and Sauces)

Wash the meats well and cut into pieces. Place in a saucepan with 3 litres (5 pints) water and bring to boil. Simmer for about 15 minutes, drain (reserving the water) and let cool.

In a large saucepan, heat the olive oil and add the dill, spring onions and lettuce. Sauté a little. Add the meat and seasonings along with the reserved water. Bring to the boil and simmer for about 20 minutes, then add the rice (if desired) and simmer until both the meat and rice are cooked.

Make the egg and lemon sauce and add to the soup. Serve hot.

Dressings and Sauces

Oil lemon dressing

125ml (4fl oz, ½ cup) extra virgin olive oil
3 tablespoons lemon juice
salt and freshly ground black pepper, to taste

Pour the oil, lemon juice and seasonings in a jar and shake until well combined. Drizzle on vegetables and salads, as needed.

Avgolemono

egg and lemon sauce

2 eggs
juice of 1 lemon
soup stock

Lightly beat the egg whites in a small bowl, add the yolks and beat a little more, then add the lemon juice gradually.

Slowly add a little stock into the egg and lemon mixture, beating all the time. Add a little more stock, continue mixing.

Pour the egg and lemon sauce into your soup or dish, stirring well so it doesn't curdle.

Olive oil and vinegar dressing

100 ml (3½ fl oz) extra
virgin olive oil
50 ml (1¾ fl oz) vinegar
salt and freshly ground black
pepper, to taste
oregano (optional)

Shake all the ingredients in a jar until well blended.
Add oregano to taste.
Drizzle on green salads or steamed vegetables.

Béchamel sauce

75 g (2½ oz, ⅓ cup) butter
45 g (1½ oz, ⅓ cup) plain
(all-purpose) flour
1 litre (1¾ pints, 4 cups)
full-fat (whole) milk,
warmed
2 eggs
salt and pepper, to taste

Melt the butter in a saucepan and stir in the flour until combined and smooth. Pour in the warm milk slowly, stirring continuously as you pour. Add the eggs and mix well. Season to taste. Stir and cook until it is of a custard consistency.

I prefer no seasoning as I like the sweetness of this sauce.

Acknowledgements

Firstly, I would like to thank my family, who had the idea for this book. Thank you for your love, support and encouragement. You know how much it all means to me, you are everything. From my heart a humble thank you.

Thank you to everyone at New Holland for saying 'yes'. To Lliane, Talina, Emma and the whole team for your vision, creativity and enthusiasm and especially for having faith in me. Thank you to Graeme for his beautiful photography and bringing my food to life and to Natasha for her creative eye. It has been so much fun.

Thank you to my Godmother, cousin and aunt and my dear dear friends for all your love and support and being there for me always along this journey.

Thank you to my family in Greece, aunts, uncles and cousins who welcomed me into their homes and into their lives with open arms and hearts. Thank you, thank you, memories that will stay with me forever.

Mum and Dad, you were the best.

To my sister, to me you will always be my little sister.

Mary x

This edition published in 2014 by
New Holland Publishers (Australia) Pty Ltd

London • Sydney • Auckland

The Chandlery Unit 114, 50 Westminster Bridge Road, London SE1 7QY, United Kingdom
1/66 Gibbes Street Chatswood NSW 2067 Australia
218 Lake Road Northcote Auckland New Zealand

ISBN: 9781742576107

Publisher: Lliane Clarke
Project editor: Talina McKenzie
Proofreader: Kay Proos
Designer: Emma Gough
Stylist: Natasha Harrison
Cook assistants: Catherine and Sarah Valle
Food photography: Graeme Gillies
Incidental photography: Mary Valle (pp4, 23, 26, 69, 82, 93, 138, 163, 193, 250), Lucy Gough (pp21, 58, 79, 106, 107, 141, 247)
Watercolour paintings: Mary Valle
Illustrations: Emma Gough and Margot Gough
Production manager: Olga Dementiev
Printer: Toppan Leefung Printing Limited (China)

Keep up with New Holland Publishers on Facebook
www.facebook.com/NewHollandPublishers

UK £16.99
US $19.99